# Rebecca Gilman
# spinning into butter

Rebecca Gilman is the recipient of the Roger L. Stevens Award from the Kennedy Center Fund for New American Plays and a Jeff Award for new work, both for *Spinning into Butter*, which premiered at the Goodman Theatre and received its New York premiere at Lincoln Center Theater. Her play *The Glory of Living* premiered at the Circle Theatre in Forest Park, Illinois, and went on to receive a Jeff Citation, an *After Dark* Award, and the American Theatre Critics Association's Osborn Award. *The Glory of Living* was produced in London at the Royal Court and subsequently received the George Devine Award and the *Evening Standard* Award for Most Promising Playwright. Ms. Gilman is also the recipient of the Scott McPherson Award and an Illinois Arts Council playwriting fellowship. Her other plays include *Boy Gets Girl*, which premiered at the Goodman Theatre, and *The Crime of the Century*.

A native of Alabama, Ms. Gilman now lives in Chicago.

# spinning into butter

## a play by
### Rebecca Gilman

Faber and Faber, Inc.
An affiliate of Farrar, Straus and Giroux / New York

Faber and Faber, Inc.
An affiliate of Farrar, Straus and Giroux
19 Union Square West, New York 10003

Library of Congress Cataloging-in-Publication Data
Gilman, Rebecca Claire.
Spinning into butter : a play / by Rebecca Gilman.—1st ed.
p. cm.
ISBN-13: 978-0-571-19984-6 (alk. paper).
ISBN-10: 0-571-19984-4
1. Universities and colleges—Drama. 2. Women deans
(Education)—Drama. 3. Vermont—Drama. 4. Racism—
Drama. I. Title.

PS3557.I456 S66 2000
812'.54—dc21                                        99-089186

Designed by Gretchen Achilles

www.fsgbooks.com

12   14   16   18   19   17   15   13

to charles

# spinning into
# butter

The world premiere of *Spinning into Butter* was presented by the Goodman Theatre in Chicago, Illinois, on May 16, 1999. The artistic director of the Goodman Theatre is Robert Falls; the executive director, Roche Schulfer. It was directed by Les Waters. Sets were designed by Linda Buchanan, costumes by Birgit Rattenborg Wise, and lighting by Robert Christen; the sound design and music were by Rob Milburn and Larry Schanker. The cast, in order of appearance, was as follows:

| | |
|---|---|
| DEAN SARAH DANIELS | *Mary Beth Fisher* |
| PATRICK CHIBAS | *Andrew Navarro* |
| ROSS COLLINS | *Jim Leaming* |
| DEAN BURTON STRAUSS | *Robert Breuler* |
| DEAN CATHERINE KENNEY | *Mary Ann Thebus* |
| MR. MEYERS | *Matt DeCaro* |
| GREG SULLIVAN | *Bruch Reed* |

*Spinning into Butter* was first produced in New York by Lincoln Center Theater (André Bishop, artistic director, and Bernard Gersten, executive producer) at the Mitzi E. Newhouse Theater on July 27, 2000, in association with Lincoln Center Festival 2000. The play was directed by Daniel Sullivan. The set was designed by John Lee Beatty, costumes by Jess Goldstein, and lighting by Brian MacDevitt; the original music and sound were by Dan Moses Schreier. The cast, in order of appearance, was as follows:

| | |
|---|---|
| DEAN SARAH DANIELS | *Hope Davis* |
| PATRICK CHIBAS | *Jai Rodriguez* |
| ROSS COLLINS | *Daniel Jenkins* |

| DEAN BURTON STRAUSS | *Henry Strozier* |
| DEAN CATHERINE KENNEY | *Brenda Wehle* |
| MR. MEYERS | *Matt DeCaro* |
| GREG SULLIVAN | *Steven Pasquale* |

## Characters

**DEAN SARAH DANIELS,** *thirty-five to forty*

**PATRICK CHIBAS,** *nineteen*

**ROSS COLLINS,** *thirty-five to forty*

**DEAN BURTON STRAUSS,** *fifty-five*

**DEAN CATHERINE KENNEY,** *sixty*

**MR. MEYERS,** *fifty*

**GREG SULLIVAN,** *twenty-one*

## Time and place

Belmont College, Belmont, Vermont, in the present

# act one

# Scene one

*A dean's office at Belmont College, a small liberal arts college in Belmont, Vermont. It is a large office, with built-in bookshelves full of books and nice white trim and a large warm rug on the floor. The desk is cluttered with papers and more books, and there are several very comfortable-looking chairs. There may even be a fireplace. Large windows provide a lot of light.*

*Sitting at the desk is* SARAH DANIELS, *who is the college's Dean of Students. She is earnest in her desire to do right by her students.*

*There is a knock at the door.*

**SARAH** Come in.

*(*PATRICK CHIBAS *enters. He is self-assured, dressed in running shorts and a T-shirt.)*

**PATRICK** Dean Daniels? I think I was next. I got a note in my box that said you wanted to see me?

**SARAH** *(Smiles.)* I left notes for a lot of students. *(*PATRICK *stares at her.)* I need you to tell me your name.

**PATRICK** Oh. Sorry. Patrick Chibas.

**SARAH** Patrick. Great. Have a seat. *(*PATRICK *takes a seat and looks around while she fishes out a file from a pile on her desk. While she looks)* Welcome back. How's moving going?

**PATRICK** Fine.

**SARAH** *(Finds his file but doesn't open it yet.)* What dorm are you in this year?

PATRICK  Grange Hall.

SARAH  Was that your first choice?

PATRICK  Last.

SARAH  I guess sophomores always get the short straw, don't
they?

PATRICK  Yeah.

SARAH  Did you go home for the summer?

PATRICK  For the first part, and then I went to Florida.

SARAH  Did you have an internship?

PATRICK  No. I just bummed around. I waited tables at the
Fish Shack.

SARAH  Just relaxed, huh?

PATRICK  Yeah. *(Small beat.)* Am I in trouble?

SARAH  No! No. I'm sorry, Patrick. I actually wanted to talk to
you about a scholarship. *(Opens his file.)*

PATRICK  Oh yeah?

SARAH  Yeah. You declared an environmental sciences major
last spring.

PATRICK  Yeah.

SARAH  Well, we have a scholarship that's designated for . . .
well, it's designated for an outstanding minority student
in environmental sciences, and I just . . . Well . . . I
wondered if you might be interested.

PATRICK  Sure.

SARAH  Good. There's just one thing, then. I need to ask you,
Patrick, on your Belmont application, you . . . Under the
voluntary disclosure of your racial/ethnic background you
marked "Other."

**Rebecca Gilman**

**PATRICK** Yeah.

**SARAH** Okay. I guess I need to know, so I can make a recommendation to the board, just what "other" is. If you don't mind.

**PATRICK** I don't mind. I'm Nuyorican.

**SARAH** Nuyorican?

**PATRICK** Yeah.

**SARAH** Huh. Would it be fair for me to say, then, that you're, um, Hispanic?

**PATRICK** I prefer Nuyorican.

**SARAH** Of course. I just . . . Well, to simplify things, when I make my recommendation to the board, do you think I could just mention that you're Hispanic?

**PATRICK** What's wrong with Nuyorican?

**SARAH** Nothing, of course.

**PATRICK** Then why don't you just say that?

**SARAH** I will. *(Beat.)* And then, I think, I'll probably be asked to explain, and I wondered, could I just explain by saying that you're Hispanic?

**PATRICK** Why would you be asked to explain?

**SARAH** Because the members of our scholarship advisory board are . . . well . . . to be honest, Patrick, they're not culturally sensitive. *(PATRICK stares at her.)* If you know what I mean.

**PATRICK** I guess I don't.

**SARAH** I think they tend to see the world in very . . . limited terms, as black or white or re . . . *(She stops herself.)* . . . racially divided along solid, clearly delineated lines.

PATRICK  So you're saying they're old?

SARAH  Yes. They're old. And they're just . . . They're not going to know what Nuyorican is.

PATRICK  *(Sighs.)* Look, you understand why I don't want to be called Hispanic, don't you?

SARAH  As I understand it, and correct me, please, if I'm wrong, it's because it really only applies to imperialists of European descent who colonized Puerto Rico.

PATRICK  Yeah. I mean, if you understand, then . . .

SARAH  Why am I suggesting it? Good question. *(Beat.)* And you're right. I shouldn't compromise your feelings for the sake of expediency. I'm sorry.

PATRICK  That's okay.

SARAH  *(Thinking)* What about Latino?

PATRICK  *(Irritated)* No.

SARAH  How 'bout just plain Puerto Rican?

PATRICK  No.

*(Beat.)*

SARAH  It's a twelve-thousand-dollar scholarship, Patrick.

PATRICK  It is?

SARAH  I want you to get it. It just seems like a shame to me to leave money sitting around in a bank when it could be doing you some good. You're a remarkably talented student and I think you should be rewarded in a meaningful way.

*(Long pause.)*

PATRICK  You can put Puerto Rican.

SARAH  *(Smiles.)* Thank you. *(She makes a note.)* I'll let you know as soon as I hear.

**PATRICK** *(Taking his cue, standing)* Okay. Sure. Thanks, Dean Daniels.

**SARAH** You're welcome. Will you send in whoever's next?

**PATRICK** Sure.

*(PATRICK opens the office door. As he does, ROSS COLLINS enters. He is an art history professor, handsome and energetic.)*

**ROSS** *(To SARAH)* Hey. *(To PATRICK)* Hi, there.

**PATRICK** Hi, Dr. Collins.

*(PATRICK exits. ROSS closes the door.)*

**ROSS** Is he one of my students?

**SARAH** I don't know.

**ROSS** Have you got a second?

**SARAH** I don't know, Ross. There are a ton of kids out there.

**ROSS** Just a second?

**SARAH** Okay. *(ROSS doesn't say anything.)* So where were you last night?

**ROSS** God, it was a nightmare. Petra's plane was five hours late and we didn't leave the city until midnight.

**SARAH** Really?

**ROSS** We just got back.

**SARAH** It took you . . . ten hours?

**ROSS** We stopped in Fort George and got a room at a motel. Petra couldn't drive and I kept nodding off, so we stopped and I got some sleep. We drove the rest of the way this morning.

**SARAH** Oh.

**ROSS** Are you angry?

**SARAH** You said you'd come by. When you got in.

ROSS  I'm sorry. I should have called.

SARAH  Well, it's not like it was prom night.

ROSS  *(Laughs.)* Prom night.

*(Beat.)*

SARAH  So how is Petra?

ROSS  She's fine, I guess. We didn't have much of a chance to talk. She fell asleep as soon as we hit the road.

SARAH  That's why she couldn't drive?

ROSS  She doesn't know how. She doesn't have a license.

SARAH  Oh.

ROSS  She grew up in Manhattan.

SARAH  Right. *(Beat.)* So how was her sabbatical?

ROSS  Amazing, apparently. She spent a few months traveling, watching dance, and then she worked with a troupe in Braunschweig who were all refugees from Bosnia. They developed an adaptation of *The Cherry Orchard*. Can you imagine? This Russian classic? These refugees from a collapsed Communist state?

SARAH  Were they Muslims or Serbs?

ROSS  I don't know. I didn't ask. Is it important?

SARAH  No, it's just, if they were Muslims . . . and then, Chekhov and Communism . . .

ROSS  And?

SARAH  I don't know. I don't get it.

ROSS  You don't?

SARAH  It seems arbitrary.

ROSS  Maybe you had to be there.

SARAH  Petra did the thing where everybody in the audience had to take off their shoes, right?

**ROSS** The piece on the pogrom. Right.

**SARAH** I didn't get that either.

**ROSS** I probably didn't do it justice.

*(Beat.)*

**SARAH** So do you want to do something tonight?

**ROSS** I don't know. *(Small beat. Grasping)* Oh God! I can't believe I almost forgot to tell you this! This is precisely what I wanted to tell you, because I knew you'd appreciate it! Okay. I got into the city at eleven or so, and I parked the car at a garage, then I decided to go to MoMA, after all, to see that Cambodian exhibit.

**SARAH** I thought you said it wasn't art.

**ROSS** It wasn't, but I wanted to see it anyway. But before I get to that, I got on the subway and it was tremendously crowded, but luckily I got a seat. So I'm sitting there, and at the next stop this man gets on and sits across from me . . . *(Gesturing)* . . . and I think to myself, I've seen this man before. And while I'm trying to place him he reaches in his coat pocket and he pulls out this small, laminated card and he holds it right here, right in front of his face, and he begins to read it silently. He's studying it furiously. So as discreetly as I could, I leaned across the aisle to see what he was reading, and while I couldn't make out the body of the text, I could make out the title, and it's something biblical. Like "John 12:24."

And so I sit back and I take another look at him. And that's when I notice that, while he's very neatly dressed, his clothes are rather shabby. His suit, for example, is too small and his shirt cuffs are fully exposed and they're stained at the edges, and the hems of his trousers are frayed, and his shoes are showing cracks in the leather. And then it hits me! The last time I was on a train in Manhattan I saw this very same man. Wearing this very same suit and reading this very same card to himself. I've been on the subway precisely four times in the past year—not since last Christmas—and twice, consecutively, I've seen this very same man. *(Beat.)* Now what are the chances of that?

SARAH  Small?

ROSS  I felt both times that he was a man about to disintegrate. A man who kept himself in one piece by a dedicated devotion to God. But a devotion that was so fragile that he literally had to keep it here, before his face, like a beacon.

*(Pause.)*

SARAH  That's precisely what you wanted to tell me?

ROSS  Don't you think it's fascinating?

SARAH  I guess it's interesting, but is that really what you wanted to tell me?

ROSS  I wanted to tell you that. Yes.

*(Beat.)*

SARAH  Did you sleep with Petra?

ROSS  *(Startled)* Last night?

SARAH  Yes.

ROSS  No. I didn't sleep with Petra last night.

SARAH  Good, then. So do you want to do something tonight?

ROSS  I can't.

SARAH  Why not?

ROSS  That's the other thing I wanted to tell you. *(Beat.* SARAH *waits.)* I really . . . I'm really sorry, but I can't keep seeing you.

**SARAH** What?

**ROSS** *(Rehearsed)* I think it's for the best. We agreed up front that we weren't working toward a permanent relationship and I think now's the time to make a break. It's a natural breaking point.

**SARAH** Why?

**ROSS** Well, the thing is this: Petra is back from her sabbatical.

**SARAH** And?

**ROSS** Well, the thing is, what I haven't told you is that before Petra left for her sabbatical, we were involved. We've been lovers for several years.

**SARAH** Lovers?

**ROSS** Or partners. Whatever you want to say.

**SARAH** And did you break up or . . . ?

**ROSS** No, we just sort of took a break. I mean, Petra was going away and we didn't know what the year would hold. So we agreed we could see other people while we were apart.

**SARAH** So . . . does Petra know about me?

**ROSS** I told her a while ago.

**SARAH** Then could you have had the decency to tell *me* about *her*?!

**ROSS** I kept meaning to, but . . . there never seemed to be a good time.

**SARAH** That's the stupidest thing I ever heard!

**ROSS** Please don't be angry.

**SARAH** So what was I, then? A temp?

**ROSS**  No, Sarah. Don't belittle yourself. You're a wonderful woman. You know that. Smart and funny and attractive.

**SARAH**  Fuck that.

**ROSS**  Please.

**SARAH**  No, I mean it. Fuck that. You don't mean that. You don't mean that about me.

**ROSS**  *(Putting his hand on her shoulder)* Sarah.

*(SARAH shrugs him off. ROSS relents. Beat.)*

**SARAH**  This is so embarrassing. Everybody must know about you and Petra.

**ROSS**  I don't know. Our friends do. The faculty. *(Beat.)* Some students.

**SARAH**  And nobody had the decency to tell me?

**ROSS**  That's the second time you've used that word, "decency."

**SARAH**  Decency is hardly a lot to expect.

**ROSS**  Look, I know I should have told you, but I couldn't bring myself to do it. You were so vulnerable.

**SARAH**  Vulnerable?

**ROSS**  You said yourself how lonely you were when you moved to Vermont, how much my company meant to you.

**SARAH**  I don't think I said that.

**ROSS**  Yes, you did.

**SARAH**  I said I could not relate to anybody on the faculty because everybody had a stupid name like Petra and nobody knew how to do anything practical like drive a car.

**ROSS**  There's no reason to say cruel things about someone you've never met.

**SARAH**  Sorry.

ROSS  Attack me. You're mad at me.

SARAH  Okay. I apologized. Now you apologize to me for
lying.

ROSS  I didn't lie.

SARAH  You did not tell me the whole truth. You equivocated,
and equivocation is the same as lying.

ROSS  That's your fundamentalist background talking.

SARAH  No no no. That's Merriam-Webster talking. *(She picks
up a dictionary and starts flipping pages.)*

ROSS  I don't need you to define the term for me.

SARAH  *(Reading)* "Equivocal."

ROSS  I'm not stupid.

SARAH  "Subject to two or more interpretations and usually
used to mislead or confuse." That's what you did. You
misled me.

ROSS  This isn't helping anything. Just . . . what matters is, I
think you're a smart, funny, and attractive woman, and I
hope we can be friends.

SARAH  Please.

ROSS  Look, we're going to run into each other all the time.
We have a committee meeting on Monday. *(Beat.* SARAH
*doesn't answer.)* Sarah. *(Beat.)* I'm really sorry. It probably
doesn't sound like I am, because I'm really . . . I'm not very
good at these things. I even practiced what I was going to
say.

SARAH  I could tell.

ROSS  Because I'm not very good at it. I never in my life
thought I'd have two girlfriends.

SARAH  Girlfriends?

**ROSS** Partners. Whatever. I never really dated until graduate school. I had bad skin. It made me shy.

**SARAH** Well, you don't have bad skin now.

**ROSS** I know! I . . . *(Realizing he's too enthusiastic)* It's just, it's been flattering. The fact that women are actually interested in me.

**SARAH** Small pond.

**ROSS** Pardon?

**SARAH** It's a small pond.

**ROSS** Oh. *(Beat.)* Well, at any rate, what I want to get across is that I really am sorry.

*(Beat.)*

**SARAH** It's okay. It's just that I don't have any friends here. That's all.

**ROSS** I'm sorry.

**SARAH** Forget it. It doesn't matter. You want to be friends?

**ROSS** I really do.

**SARAH** Fine. We're friends.

**ROSS** Great. *(He pulls* SARAH *into a hug, which she tolerates, releases her.)* Well. You've got a hundred students waiting to see you.

**SARAH** Yes, I do.

**ROSS** *(At the door)* Do you want to have lunch one day this week? Wednesday?

**SARAH** Why don't you call me.

**ROSS** Okay.

**SARAH** Okay. *(He opens the door and exits. She crosses to the open door and makes a motion to a student we can't* *see.)* Hold on. I just need to make a phone call. *(She closes the door and leans her back against it.)* Christ. *(She stands for a moment. The chimes on the chapel next door sound their tune, then begin to count out the hour. It is ten o'clock. Somewhere in the middle, she gathers herself and turns and opens her office door.)* Okay. Next?

## Scene two

*A week later. Sarah's office.* DEAN CATHERINE KENNEY, BURTON STRAUSS, *Chair of the Humanities Department, and* ROSS *are in the middle of a heated argument.*

STRAUSS  If we require courses, then it's not flexible.

KENNEY  Of course it's flexible. They're taking classes in a dozen departments.

STRAUSS  But why institutionalize it?

KENNEY  Because we're an institution. If we don't impose guidelines, then the students can just come in here, take what they want, and graduate.

ROSS  Isn't that what they do already?

KENNEY  Of course not. We make demands on them.

ROSS  Like those winter term classes?

STRAUSS  Exactly.

KENNEY  Exactly what?

STRAUSS  "The Films of Brigitte Bardot"? I'd hardly call that a demanding class.

**KENNEY**  Winter term is an exception.

**ROSS**  Why?

**KENNEY**  Because. It's only one month. In the winter.

**STRAUSS**  But why should they waste it?

**KENNEY**  Because. *(Beat.)* That's when they ski. All right?

**STRAUSS**  What?

**KENNEY**  Sixty-seven percent of students surveyed said that the ski slope was a deciding factor in choosing Belmont over competing colleges.

*(ROSS laughs.)*

**STRAUSS**  I should have known.

**ROSS**  Okay. Should we vote on the courses?

**KENNEY**  We don't have a quorum without Sarah. We'll have to wait.

**STRAUSS**  But she'll vote with you and we'll have a tie. She always does.

**KENNEY**  She sees things from my point of view.

**STRAUSS**  The marketing point of view. You'd turn the library into a Cineplex if you thought it'd attract more students.

**KENNEY**  Would not.

**STRAUSS**  You'll have me teaching Aristotle as he applies to Seinfeld.

**KENNEY**  Will not.

**STRAUSS**  I'm not David Letterman.

**KENNEY**  We know.

**STRAUSS**  At any rate, I don't think it should be left up to Sarah. Don't I get some votes by proxy?

**KENNEY**  Why should you?

**STRAUSS**  As Chair?

**KENNEY**  No. We'll have to wait. *(Long pause. She looks around.)* Does her office seem bigger than mine?

**STRAUSS**  No.

**KENNEY**  I think it's bigger.

**STRAUSS**  I don't think it is.

**KENNEY**  I'm going to walk it off. *(She crosses to a wall and begins walking the distance.)* One . . . two . . . three . . .

**STRAUSS**  There's just less stuff in it.

**KENNEY**  You can't tell with these colonial buildings. Everything's irregular.

**STRAUSS**  They were master craftsmen.

**KENNEY**  Put a marble on that floor and it will roll straight to the corner.

**STRAUSS**  It's an old building. It's settled.

**KENNEY**  Do it.

**ROSS**  Please. Could we at least discuss scheduling for the spring? Something pertinent.

**KENNEY**  *(Finishes walking the length of the wall.)* Oh, fine! It's not bigger at all. It's smaller.

**STRAUSS**  See.

**KENNEY**  See what? *(SARAH enters, hurriedly.)* You're late.

**SARAH**  I'm sorry. There's been a . . . There's a problem.

**KENNEY**  What?

**SARAH**  Someone's been leaving threatening . . . well, racist notes on the door of one of our African American students.

**KENNEY**  Please tell me you're kidding.

**ROSS**  *(Overlapping)* Oh my God.

**SARAH**  Maybe you should look at them. *(She holds out two notes. They gather around and read, passing them among* *themselves. As they read)* He said he was willing to ignore the first one, but then he found this one this afternoon and it was so . . . graphic.

*(Pause. They read, silenced. Then)*

ROSS  God.

KENNEY  And you say somebody just left this on his door?

SARAH  Yes. When he got the second one, he took them over to security and they called me.

KENNEY  Which dorm is he in?

SARAH  Houghton Hall. He's a freshman.

KENNEY  I've never seen anything like this before.

SARAH  His name is Simon Brick.

ROSS  Is he all right? Is he frightened?

SARAH  I don't know. I haven't talked to him yet. He left the notes and went on to class.

KENNEY  Do you think we should call him over? I could send somebody to his class . . .

SARAH  I left a message asking him to come see me when he gets in. If he wanted to go to class, I thought we should let him. Whatever's easiest for him is what I was thinking. *(Beat.)* He doesn't even have a roommate.

KENNEY  He has a single?

SARAH  There are those two in Houghton.

KENNEY  I thought they were reserved for sophomores.

SARAH  We can't get sophomores to live in a freshman dorm.

STRAUSS  *(Who's been studying the notes)* Rooming accommodations? Is this what you want to talk about?

SARAH  I just thought you would want to know something about him.

**Rebecca Gilman**

STRAUSS Yes, yes, but first we have to decide what to do. *(Indicating the notes)* We have a dangerous racist in our midst.

KENNEY I suppose someone from security could watch his dorm, or if he wants to—

STRAUSS *(Interrupting, overlapping)* No no no. The question is: How do we punish this racist?

SARAH Won't we expel him?

ROSS Or her.

STRAUSS *(Overlapping)* That's a defensive action. We have to be pro-active on this. We must make it known, loud and clear, that this sentiment, this trash, is not Belmont. That Belmont cannot be reduced to this outrageous action. We should issue some sort of statement right away, condemning this—

SARAH *(Interrupting)* I think we should try to find out who did it first, before we go around issuing statements.

KENNEY Technically I should call President Garvey and ask him what to do.

ROSS Garvey won't know what to do. He's so out of touch. Burton's right. I think we should make a public gesture of some sort. We should call a campus-wide meeting so we can discuss what's going on.

STRAUSS Yes.

SARAH Don't you think we should talk to Simon first?

ROSS Look, we pride ourselves on our inclusiveness. We claim to embrace cultural diversity. And yet some racist is running loose on campus, and I would wager that this idiot is very much like all our other students in appearance and manner and class, and that's what we need to reveal. That racism isn't somebody else's problem. It's our problem. If we handle this right, it could be a real learning experience for the students.

KENNEY All right, then. Good. This seems like the sort of response we should have, doesn't it? If it leaks out to any of the parents and some irate mother calls me, I can say, "We've already organized a campus meeting in order to reduce any stress or obviate any adverse reactions . . ." Something like that.

STRAUSS Obviate? Will that translate?

KENNEY Whatever. I'll write it out so it sounds right. I always get fifteen or twenty calls on these sorts of things and it's better just to write down what you plan to say.

SARAH I thought you'd never seen anything like this before.

KENNEY Not like this, no. So, shall I propose this campus forum thingee to President Garvey? I'll tell him everyone at the committee meeting thinks it's a good idea. He doesn't have to know that we're missing half the people.

ROSS I strongly recommend it. You can tell him that.

STRAUSS As do I.

KENNEY Sarah?

SARAH I just . . . I feel like we're moving too fast. We should talk to Simon first. What if he doesn't want us to talk about him this way?

STRAUSS Why wouldn't he?

SARAH I just think it might be embarrassing for him. *(They don't get it.)* He's very quiet. Everyone would stare.

**STRAUSS** No one will stare.

**KENNEY** All right, then. We should put out a memo to the faculty before we call the students together. Ross?

**ROSS** I'll be glad to write something up. Burton?

**STRAUSS** I'll be glad to help.

*(A knock on the door.)*

**KENNEY** and **SARAH** Come in.

*(MR. MEYERS, an older security guard, enters, carrying a plastic bag.)*

**MEYERS** Oh. Excuse me.

**SARAH** It's all right, Mr. Meyers. What is it?

**MEYERS** The police said we should put the notes in this bag to protect the fingerprints.

**KENNEY** The police! You didn't call the police, Sarah?

**SARAH** Yes.

**KENNEY** Never do that!

**SARAH** I—

**KENNEY** It'll be in the local press and then the wire services pick it up and then we're everybody's business! Really! How could you be so stupid?

**SARAH** I thought since the note was so violent . . .

**KENNEY** It's an internal incident. Internal. You've seriously overstepped your bounds here, Sarah.

**SARAH** I thought I was fully authorized—

**KENNEY** *(Overlapping)* I'm not going to quibble with you. I've *got* to call Garvey now.

**MEYERS** The police are waiting for you in your office. They wanted to talk to somebody in charge.

**KENNEY** And you thought that was me, did you?

(*KENNEY exits and* MEYERS *follows.*)

**STRAUSS** I was wondering who we should get to lead the forum.

**ROSS** I'd like to put my own name in.

**STRAUSS** As would I, of course. Everyone will want to have their say.

**SARAH** I thought that was the point.

**ROSS** It is.

**SARAH** I still think we should wait.

**STRAUSS** But you didn't say anything to convince us, did you. You're not going to persuade until you learn to argue effectively. But they don't teach you social workers how to argue, they only teach you how to console.

**SARAH** I'm not a social worker.

**STRAUSS** Ayn Rand was right about your lot. (*He laughs.*) Come down to my office, Ross, and let's draft that memo.

**ROSS** I'll be right there.

(*ROSS and* STRAUSS *exchange looks.*)

**STRAUSS** Oh. Right. Good luck with Simon Brick, Sarah. Let us know how it goes.

(*STRAUSS exits.* ROSS *looks at* SARAH *and closes the door.*)

**ROSS** You did the right thing, calling the police.

**SARAH** No shit. (*Small beat.*) I mean, thanks.

**ROSS** Hey. What are you doing Saturday night?

**SARAH** (*Brightening a little*) Um . . . nothing, I guess. Why?

**ROSS** I was wondering . . . Well, a few years ago, Petra and I began hosting salons. It's just an informal get-together.

**Rebecca Gilman**

People read what they've been working on, or bring some artwork, or whatever. Anyway, we're having one this Saturday and we were wondering, would you like to come?

SARAH  A salon with you and Petra?

ROSS  Yes.

SARAH  Boy. You know? I'd rather have my eyeballs gouged out with soup spoons.

ROSS  *(Smiles.)* Well, then. *(Beat.)* How violent your opinions are when they don't matter.

SARAH  Wait a minute. You and Petra live together?

ROSS  Yes.

SARAH  In your house?

ROSS  Yes.

SARAH  Where were her things?

ROSS  You're still mad at me, aren't you?

SARAH  Her little ballet shoes. Her tutus?

ROSS  She doesn't wear tutus.

SARAH  *(Grabs a book from the shelf and shoves it at him.)* Take this book you gave me. Take it back.

ROSS  *(Takes it, looks.)* The Rilke? Sarah. You have to keep the Rilke. *(He puts it on her desk.)* Look, I should have told you that Petra and I lived together, but I didn't want to tell you that we were *seeing* each other, so I . . . *(He trails off.)*

SARAH  Fucked me over?

ROSS  That's not what I was going to say. *(Beat.)* Look, let's talk about this later, when you're not so angry. *(SARAH doesn't answer.)* Just . . . read the Rilke.

*(He leaves. Immediately* SARAH *takes up the Rilke and throws it at the door. A loud thud.)*

MEYERS  *(From offstage)* Hello?

SARAH  Hello?

*(*MEYERS *cracks the door open.)*

MEYERS  Hello?

SARAH  Come in. *(*MEYERS *enters.)* Yes?

MEYERS  The police took the notes.

SARAH  What'd they say?

MEYERS  They think it was a student. Nobody from town would really know there was a black kid in that particular room.

SARAH  That makes sense, I guess.

MEYERS  They said they'd take fingerprints off them.

SARAH  We all touched them.

MEYERS  Yeah. They said they'd maybe ask for some hand-writing samples. Just for comparison.

SARAH  Whose?

MEYERS  Other students in the dorm, prob'ly. *(*SARAH *nods, distracted.)* Are you okay?

SARAH  It's been a bad day.

MEYERS  *(Picks up the Rilke.)* You dropped your book.

SARAH  I threw my book.

MEYERS  You don't like it?

SARAH  Actually, no, I've always hated Rilke.

MEYERS  *(Nods.)* It's sort of small. I find I feel better if I throw heavy things. Maybe a dictionary. Or a thesaurus. *(*SARAH *laughs.)* Here. *(He hands her the book.)* I've worked here twenty years, Sarah, and one thing I've learned, these people don't know their ass from a hole in the ground. (SARAH *laughs again.*) After twenty years, you find it's not so funny. (SARAH *stops laughing.*) See what I mean?

## Scene three

*Two weeks later.* SARAH *is talking to* GREG SULLIVAN, *a senior.* GREG *is very much the Belmont man. He is handsome, self-assured, well educated.*

GREG I guess when we heard about the thing with the notes, we were shocked, but it seemed like something happening outside of our daily experience. You know? I mean, it wasn't that we couldn't relate to it, it's that it was almost so horrific that it made us numb. Does that make any sense? Like we didn't want to even contemplate that one of us could have done it.

SARAH Well, of course, we still don't know who did do it.

GREG I know, but really, it's probably somebody in his dorm. Don't you think?

SARAH We really don't know yet.

GREG Anyway, though, my point is that we were just going along, I think, not really wanting to face the reality of the situation. But then, last night, when Dean Strauss got up and said to, you know, look inside ourselves and see were we culpable at all, well, that's what really hit me, I guess. Because we still were acting like something outside was responsible. Instead of something inside. Which is what hit me. You know? It's in here. Inside.

SARAH  Well, I'm glad it started you thinking. That's what the meeting was for, I guess.

GREG  I think everyone came out of it really energized. I mean, just on my hall, we sat up until like three or four in the morning talking about it. About racism and how it had affected us, or not affected us, as the case may be. I mean, where I'm from, I don't think people are racist. But then I didn't think anyone at Belmont was racist either.

SARAH  Where are you from?

GREG  Greenwich, Connecticut.

SARAH  Right.

GREG  But really, my point is that we were all geared up to talk last night, but today is another day and I know how people are. If we're not careful, we'll just drop it. So the thing is this: I want to start an organization. I want to call it Students for Tolerance. I want us to get together so we can keep talking like we were last night.

SARAH  I think that sounds like a fine idea.

GREG  Excellent!

(Pause.)

SARAH  So what would you like me to do for you, Greg?

GREG  Well, I thought I might go ahead and call a meeting for next week.

SARAH  Do you need a space?

GREG  That would be good.

SARAH  *(Opens a three-ring binder on her desk.)* You can
   have Scott Auditorium, Monday at seven.

GREG  Terrific. And I'd like to put up posters announcing it.

SARAH  Go right ahead.

GREG  Well, this is what I was wondering. Is there any money
   the college could give us, to defray expenses?

SARAH  Of course. You'll need to go to the Student Activities
   Committee.

GREG  And they'll just give it to me?

SARAH  Well, you'll need to fill out some forms. You need to
   be approved as an official organization. And you'll need a
   sponsor. But I bet if you asked Dean Strauss, he'd be glad
   to sponsor you.

GREG  I don't know. This all seems so complicated all of a
   sudden.

SARAH  It's a little bit of work up front, but I think it's worth
   it.

GREG  You're right, of course. It's just . . . Well, how long
   would it take to get funding?

SARAH  Probably six weeks.

GREG  Man.

SARAH  I know it seems like a long time, but if you wanted to
   go ahead and meet in the meantime, you can get the
   posters yourself and the committee will reimburse you.
   *(Beat.)* So if I were you, Greg, I'd go see Dean Strauss first.
   *(Beat.)*

GREG  This wouldn't . . . I mean, well, would it look bad if I
   said I was president of Students for Tolerance before
   the committee actually approved it?

SARAH  Bad to whom?

GREG  Well, I mean, to be perfectly honest, I'm applying to
law school and the résumé is a little thin, if you know what
I mean. I mean, something like this would definitely add a
line.

SARAH  I see.

*(Beat.)*

GREG  So do you think it would look bad?

SARAH  I really couldn't say. Would anyone question it?

GREG  I don't know. If they did, though, if they called the
college . . .

SARAH  I can't advise you on this, Greg. I think this is up to
you to decide.

GREG  Oh. *(Beat.)* I mean, of course.

SARAH  I hope this doesn't dampen your enthusiasm for the
idea.

GREG  Absolutely not. I'm committed to this. I am. Now, if I
can just figure out how to dig up some cash for these
posters.

SARAH  Are you in a fraternity?

GREG  Yeah.

SARAH  Well, each fraternity's charter calls for a certain
percentage of dues to be spent on service-oriented
activities.

GREG  They do?

SARAH  Yes, they do. They could pay for your posters.

*(Beat.)*

GREG  I don't know. It just doesn't seem like the kind of thing
they'd go in for. I mean, would they even know what I

was talking about? That's the question. Not to doubt you, of course, but I never heard of this fund or whatever before and I actually manage to stay awake during those informational meetings.

*(GREG laughs. SARAH doesn't.)*

SARAH  Greg, I'm intimately familiar with each fraternity's charter.

GREG  I'm sure you are. *(Beat.)* I mean, somebody around here is, obviously. Right? I mean, that's why we're going coed, isn't it?

SARAH  Yes. It is.

GREG  *(Laughs uncomfortably.)* That was kind of a shock, when I first heard that. Coed fraternities. *(Beat.)* But really, the point was well taken. There are no sororities on campus. The women have no options. *(He laughs again, then studies SARAH.)* That was you, wasn't it, that started all the stir.

SARAH  Yes.

GREG  Dean Daniels. I'm sure I'd heard your name, but I'd forgotten. Well. Congratulations on a job well done.

SARAH  Thank you.

GREG  *(Standing)* But rather than appeal to Tau Omega, I think I'll take your first piece of advice and go to the Student Activities Committee. I can wait. And I can shell out a few bucks for posters, too, if it's something I believe in.

SARAH  And you do.

GREG  And I do. *(Beat.)* Excellent, then. *(Offering his hand)* You've been a great help.

*(SARAH shakes his hand.)*

SARAH  That's why they pay me.

# Scene four

*Sarah's office, later that day.* SARAH *and* ROSS *are talking.*

ROSS  Things just aren't the same. We're not communicating. At first I thought she just needed time to readjust to being home, but it's been two weeks now and we've hardly had a conversation. Whenever I start talking to her, she just looks away, and when I ask her what she's thinking about, she says, "Nothing."

SARAH  Did she meet somebody over in Europe?

ROSS  That's not what I'm saying.

SARAH  I was just thinking that maybe she had sex with somebody over in Europe and maybe she's thinking about that person she had sex with over in Europe.

ROSS  I thought you were willing to talk to me about this.

SARAH  I am. I'm talking to you.

ROSS  You're punishing me. This isn't how a friend would respond to my problems.

SARAH  Sorry. *(Beat.)* Maybe she's just pissed off that you had sex with somebody. Maybe you hurt her feelings.

ROSS  We had an agreement.

SARAH  Maybe she didn't actually expect you to take her up on it.

ROSS  You think she's jealous.

SARAH  I bet no matter what Petra says about the bourgeois constraints of traditional notions of commitment, or the bourgeois constraints of shoes, that she's pissed off and she's punishing you.

**ROSS**  She would never tell me if she was. She's really passive-aggressive. *(Switching gears)* Now then, I'm supposed to reserve Ingersoll Chapel for our next forum.

**SARAH**  You are? *(She reaches for a binder.)*

**ROSS**  Tuesday night. I hope it's free, because we've already posted it.

**SARAH**  I didn't realize you were having another one.

**ROSS**  Is it free?

**SARAH**  Yes. *(She makes a note.)* There. Tuesday night. Race forum.

**ROSS**  What's wrong?

**SARAH**  Nothing.

**ROSS**  You don't think we should have another one?

**SARAH**  I didn't say that.

**ROSS**  What, then?

**SARAH**  I just think that if you're going to have another one, you should come up with a recommendation or something, so that something tangible comes out of it instead of everybody standing around talking about how bad racism is. Because we already know that racism is bad.

**ROSS**  A recommendation?

**SARAH**  Yeah.

**ROSS**  Like what?

**SARAH**  I don't know. Stop being stupid.

**ROSS**  Stop being stupid?

**SARAH**  Yeah. Stop being stupid. Stop acting like you know the first thing about black people. Stop thinking you have black friends just because you get along really well with your maid.

**ROSS** That's what the forums are for, though. To help these kids understand a different range of experience.

**SARAH** I'm sure that's your intent.

**ROSS** But?

**SARAH** But in my humble opinion, all you do is talk about racism and then you have this collective sigh of white guilt and then everybody feels better and then they drive downtown in their Saabs and buy sweaters.

**ROSS** So you think the forums provide a sort of cheap penance?

**SARAH** Yes.

**ROSS** Well, I don't agree. I think they're very productive.

**SARAH** Fine. I don't.

**ROSS** *(Considers her.)* You know, I like the way we're talking to each other. I think maybe, when we were dating, you were holding back a little, avoiding conflict.

**SARAH** Just out of some insane desire to get along.

**ROSS** That's terrible.

**SARAH** If it'll make you feel any better, I'll drop all tact in the future.

**ROSS** Excellent. Well, I'm off. *(He opens the door to leave. From offstage, we hear* STRAUSS's *voice.)*

**STRAUSS** *(From offstage)* Ross!

**ROSS** Fuck. *(Muttering to* SARAH*)* Ever since he had that thought piece published in the *Times*, he's just insufferable. *(To* STRAUSS, *offstage)* Burton, hello!

*(*STRAUSS *appears at the door.)*

**STRAUSS** Hello there. How are you?

**ROSS**  Fine.

**STRAUSS**  Did you see the latest *Harper's*?

**ROSS**  No, why?

**STRAUSS**  There was an article in there by David Foster.
Wasn't he a classmate of yours?

**ROSS**  Yes. *(Beat.)* Was it any good?

**STRAUSS**  Quite good, really.

**ROSS**  Is he still harping on that authenticity thing?

**STRAUSS**  It was a piece on outsider art. Yes.

**ROSS**  Please.

**STRAUSS**  How are you, Sarah?

**SARAH**  Fine.

**ROSS**  I wonder if David's still fat.

**STRAUSS**  Look, I need to talk to you both about something.
*(He comes in and closes the door.)* This young man, Greg
Sullivan, has approached me about sponsoring a
Students for Tolerance group.

**ROSS**  What's this?

**SARAH**  A student group. For tolerance.

**STRAUSS**  It's an excellent idea, I think. A direct result of our
forum. And I'm happy to do it, though really, Sarah, I was
surprised that you recommended me.

**SARAH**  You seemed like an obvious choice to me.

**STRAUSS**  Well, thank you. We're having our first meeting on
Monday night, and the thing is this: we would like Simon
Brick to attend.

**SARAH**  I don't think he can come.

**STRAUSS**  I understand that he's shy.

SARAH  He's quiet.

STRAUSS  But we're a small group and we would be honored
to include him as a member.

SARAH  He didn't want to come to the forum, Burton. I doubt
he'd want to come to this.

ROSS  I wish he had come.

SARAH  I supported his decision not to come.

STRAUSS  To whom?

SARAH  To him.

ROSS  I guess I can see how it might be intimidating, facing
such a large crowd.

SARAH  I don't think it has anything to do with crowds.

ROSS  He's an only child, though, isn't he?

SARAH  I don't know.

STRAUSS  Maybe it's the cultural mix.

SARAH  What?

STRAUSS  He attended a predominantly African American
school, didn't he? In Philadelphia?

ROSS  I thought he was from Bucks County.

SARAH  Pittsburgh. And I don't know what the racial mix was.

ROSS  But it was a public school.

SARAH  It was a Catholic school.

STRAUSS  Oh. I didn't realize he was Catholic.

SARAH  I don't know if he is or not. Is it important?

STRAUSS  No, no. Still, I'd like him to come.

ROSS  If Sarah's going to ask him to do something, she should
ask him to come to the second forum.

STRAUSS  Ask him to do both. You could persuade him. You're
very good with the students.

**SARAH** Because I'm a social worker?

**STRAUSS** What?

**SARAH** Ayn Rand knew what to do with my sort . . .

**STRAUSS** *(Laughs.)* Oh. That. You didn't take me seriously,
did you?

**SARAH** Yes.

**STRAUSS** You don't really think that I subscribe to Ayn Rand?
*(He laughs some more.)* Goodness.

*(Beat.)*

**SARAH** I'm not going to ask him to do anything, Burton. If it's
so important to you, you can always ask him yourself.

**STRAUSS** I suppose I could. You say he lives in Houghton
Hall?

**SARAH** Yes.

**STRAUSS** I don't think I've been in a dorm since I was in college myself. I always hated the dormitories.

**SARAH** You could call if you don't want to go over.

**STRAUSS** Do they have their own phones now or would it
ring in the hallway?

**SARAH** They have their own phones. And electricity, too.

**STRAUSS** What?

**ROSS** She's making a joke.

**STRAUSS** Oh. You say he's very shy?

**SARAH** No. He's quiet, but I don't think he's shy.

**STRAUSS** Maybe we could write him a note. *(To ROSS)* Do you
want to help me write a note?

**ROSS** I'd be glad to.

**SARAH** You should do that, then. *(A knock on the door.)* Yes?

*(MEYERS enters.)*

**MEYERS** I'm sorry. I didn't realize you had company.

**SARAH** It's all right. We're finished.

**ROSS** Come on, Burton, let's go. Thanks, Sarah.

**SARAH** Sure.

*(They leave.* MEYERS *closes the door behind them.)*

**MEYERS** Simon got another note. *(He pulls a note from his pocket and hands it to* SARAH.*)*

**SARAH** *(Looking at the note, reading)* "Little Black Sambo . . ." *(Beat.)* Is he in his room now? *(*MEYERS *nods.)* Let's take this to Dean Kenney, and then I'll go talk to him.

**MEYERS** Okay.

*(They turn to leave as* PATRICK CHIBAS *enters the open door.)*

**SARAH** Hi, Patrick.

**PATRICK** Could I talk to you?

**SARAH** This is kind of a bad time. Can we make it tomorrow?

**PATRICK** My dad said I should insist on talking to you. Now.

**SARAH** Okay. *(She looks at* MEYERS.*)*

**MEYERS** I'll wait outside.

**SARAH** Thank you.

*(*MEYERS *exits, closing the door behind him.)*

**PATRICK** We got this letter from the financial aid office. *(He holds out a letter to* SARAH. *Before she can take it)* When I got the scholarship they took away my financial aid. It's costing more now.

**SARAH** That's not right. Let me see.

**PATRICK** My dad is furious. He was already mad about the whole Hispanic thing.

**SARAH** He was?

**PATRICK** Especially after I told him about this thing with

Simon Brick. He was so pissed, but I told him that you were just . . . you know, trying to help us out. But this isn't helping us out. You know? I mean . . . I don't know.

SARAH  I'll have to call the financial aid office.

PATRICK  This was supposed to be a scholarship.

SARAH  It is a scholarship. There's been some misunderstanding.

PATRICK  I really got my hopes up. I thought my dad would finally stop complaining about how much this place costs.

SARAH  You tell your dad that if he wants to complain, to call me. You deserve that scholarship and I'm going to straighten this out. Okay?

PATRICK  Okay. *(Beat. He doesn't leave.)*

SARAH  What is it?

PATRICK  Well, some of my friends asked me to talk to you about something else.

SARAH  Yeah?

PATRICK  We felt like that meeting thing we had to go to was really insulting.

SARAH  The forum?

PATRICK  Yeah. We felt like it was really patronizing. You know?

SARAH  You mean the minority students?

PATRICK  What? All my friends are "minorities"?

SARAH  Of course not. I just thought that's what you meant.

PATRICK  Why? Because "Hispanic" people stick together?

SARAH  No, no. I didn't mean like, you and your "amigos" or anything. *(She smiles.)* That was a joke. I was trying to diffuse the tension with a joke.

**PATRICK** It wasn't funny.

**SARAH** I'm sorry. I just . . . it's just that you said you felt the forum was patronizing and I thought, To whom would it be most patronizing? and then I thought, To the minority students, and so I said that. I mean, I agree. It was patronizing. To the minority students.

**PATRICK** You know, I didn't correct you before, when I was in here before, but it's "students of color," not "minority students."

**SARAH** Students of color. God. Sorry. Of course. That's what I meant to say. The "minority" thing, it's just a technical thing.

**PATRICK** What does that mean?

**SARAH** Just, you know, paperwork . . . everything has to fit into a box. It's an administrative thing. I'm sorry. I stand corrected. *(Beat.)* So. Everybody thought it was patronizing. The forum.

**PATRICK** Most of us did, yeah.

**SARAH** So why did you find it patronizing?

**PATRICK** Because. The students of color were being talked about like we weren't even there, like we couldn't even talk for ourselves. And the white kids were being talked about like they were all criminals. I mean, I think Dean Strauss managed to offend everybody in the audience. *(*SARAH *laughs.)* You were up there, too, onstage.

**SARAH** But I didn't say anything.

**PATRICK** But you were up there.

**SARAH** Right. *(Beat.)* So essentially, you felt you were being robbed of your agency.

**PATRICK**  I probably wouldn't use that particular expression,
like that. But I'd say yeah. Basically it felt like I didn't exist.

**SARAH**  So would you feel comfortable saying that? At the
next forum?

**PATRICK**  They're gonna have another one?

**SARAH**  Tuesday night. Why don't you go? Tell Dean Strauss
what you told me and explain how it makes you feel. I
think your voice really matters.

**PATRICK**  Really? It matters?

**SARAH**  Of course.

**PATRICK**  I was being sarcastic.

**SARAH**  Oh.

**PATRICK**  Making a joke to diffuse the tension.

**SARAH**  Got me.

**PATRICK**  Yeah.

**SARAH**  Look, don't let my . . . um . . . whatever . . . stop you
from going.

**PATRICK**  Don't worry. I'll be there.

**SARAH**  Good. *(Beat.)* Now, about the scholarship, just tell
your father that he doesn't have to worry. I'll take care of it.
Tell him you'll be paying less than you would at a state
school.

**PATRICK**  I'll tell him that.

**SARAH**  He should be very proud of you. There aren't many
scholarships this size. It's really an honor. (PATRICK *nods,
unimpressed.)* Look, Patrick, I really am on your side.
You're an exceptional student, and you're obviously very
smart and very talented. I'm sorry if I've offended you.

**PATRICK**  You've apologized already.

SARAH  And as my dad used to say, "You can't put that in the bank."

PATRICK  That's not what I meant.

SARAH  *(Quickly)* No, it's okay if you did. It's okay. So let me give you twelve thousand dollars. Because that's something you can put in the bank. Okay?

PATRICK  *(Beat. Accepting it)* Okay.


# Scene five

*Sarah's office, the next week. She is on the phone.*


SARAH  I guess, I mean, if you wanted to eat waffles in the middle of the day, I don't see anything wrong with that. *(Beat.)* Well, yeah, I would say heat them up at least. *(Beat.)* I'm fine . . . *(Beat. Different tone)* I am. It's just . . . it seems like, you know, I keep calling you earlier in the day, and you're drinking earlier in the day. *(Beat.)* Well, we had a deal, you know, that we wouldn't talk when you were drunk, and now I'm wondering, you know, when is that? . . . What's that beeping? . . . Well, don't answer it . . . I don't care, let them call back— Mom!— *(She puts the phone back to her ear, resigned to waiting.* STRAUSS *knocks on the door and sticks his head in.)* I'm on the phone.

STRAUSS  It's really urgent.

SARAH  I'm on the phone.

STRAUSS  Simon Brick must come to the next forum.

SARAH  So you can yell at him?

STRAUSS  None of that would have happened last night if Simon had been there.

SARAH  I don't follow. *(Back on phone quickly. She holds up her hand to* STRAUSS *to get him to shut up. Trying to keep her voice low)* Are you there? *(Beat. On phone)* Well, why did you tell her? Don't tell her what I said. *(Beat. On phone)* Can I call you later? *(Beat.)* Okay. I— *(Beat.)* No, I'm sorry. *(Beat. On phone)* I love you, too. *(She hangs up.)*

STRAUSS  Family?

SARAH  My mother.

STRAUSS  I could tell. I'm the same way with my mother. It's like I'm twelve again.

*(Beat. They study one another.)*

SARAH  I'm sorry, Burton, what did you want?

STRAUSS  I just feel that the students wouldn't have attacked me last night if Simon had been there.

SARAH  How could Simon have prevented it?

STRAUSS  If he were there and they could see that I support him and they could see . . .

SARAH  A black person onstage with you?

STRAUSS  A united front.

SARAH  Well, that might be part of the problem, I suppose, but I think an even larger part of the problem is that you yelled at them. They were just trying to explain their feelings and you lit into them.

STRAUSS  They were questioning my motivations! My intentions! Which are flawless!

SARAH  All they said was that your manner was patronizing.

**STRAUSS**  Which implies that I'm racist! *(Beat.)* This is very upsetting to me.

**SARAH**  I can see that.

**STRAUSS**  I've never been criticized like this before.

**SARAH**  Well, I don't think that it was completely outrageous.

**STRAUSS**  Oh?

**SARAH**  Well, you do have a kind of Old World manner about you. You know?

**STRAUSS**  Oh, this is precious.

**SARAH**  Not to hurt your feelings, but . . .

**STRAUSS**  Coming from you!

**SARAH**  What's that supposed to mean?

**STRAUSS**  You're a fucking bureaucrat! A clerk!

**SARAH**  I'm sorry?

**STRAUSS**  "Have a nice day." "Come back and see us." You may as well be working at a bank!

**SARAH**  *(Stares, befuddled.)* I just . . . How did we get here?

**STRAUSS**  I want Simon Brick!

**SARAH**  Then ask him!

**STRAUSS**  He wouldn't answer our note!

**SARAH**  Then leave him alone!

*(DEAN KENNEY comes in.)*

**KENNEY**  What is all the yelling?

**STRAUSS**  I need her help, she won't give it to me.

**KENNEY**  What do you need, Burton?

**STRAUSS**  I need Simon Brick to come to the forum, to tell them I'm not a racist.

**KENNEY**  I don't think that's a good idea.

**STRAUSS**  But I—

**KENNEY** I know you're upset, I know how much this hurts you, to be attacked, especially when your character is flawless.

**STRAUSS** Yes!

**KENNEY** But I don't think it's a good idea to have someone speak for you. You have to speak for yourself, Burton. Tell them of your record, your impeccable record, and let them see for themselves what sort of man you are. *(He considers.)* Go and write it out. Only you can do this.

**STRAUSS** Of course. Of course, you're right. What am I doing, coming to her?

**KENNEY** She's our liaison to the minority students. That's why you came to her. But you don't really need Sarah's help. You need time to ruminate, and then time to compose.

**STRAUSS** Of course. You're right. *(Gives a little giggle.)* I get so worked up.

**KENNEY** Go on, then.

**STRAUSS** All right, Catherine. Thank you. *(He gives her a peck on the cheek and hurries off.)*

**SARAH** What was that about?

**KENNEY** Burton and I, you know, have had something of a tortured relationship for a long while. It ceased to be sexual some time ago, but we still have deep feelings for one another, and really and truly, I think I may be the only person in the world who fully understands him. He's very vulnerable.

*(Pause.* SARAH *stares.)*

**SARAH** I just meant, what was that about my being a liaison to the minority students.

KENNEY  Oh well, because of the Lancaster thing.

SARAH  Pardon?

KENNEY  Well, you know we consciously set out to diversify, and we really wanted your experience, coming from Lancaster. Serving a more . . . diverse student population.

SARAH  It wasn't really diverse.

KENNEY  Then a minority population.

SARAH  *I* was in the minority.

KENNEY  Then an African American population. Is that what you want me to say?

SARAH  I don't want you to say anything. It's just that it was a fluke that I was there in the first place. They needed a last-minute replacement. My dissertation adviser recommended me.

KENNEY  But you must have specialized, or expressed an interest . . .

SARAH  I did at one point, yes. *(Beat.)* So you wanted someone who had worked with students of color.

KENNEY  Yes.

SARAH  That was never made clear to me. *(Pause.)* Why didn't you hire a black person, then?

KENNEY  Well . . . I'll be honest, we did try.

SARAH  You couldn't get anybody.

KENNEY  We had someone in mind, but he took another offer. I think he wanted more money. And I don't think he really wanted to live in Vermont.

SARAH  I did want to live in Vermont.

KENNEY  We're a good match, then.

*(Pause.)*

**SARAH**  So when I came here for my interview, were you surprised?

**KENNEY**  Surprised?

**SARAH**  Because I was white?

**KENNEY**  Oh. No.

**SARAH**  So you didn't think that because I'd been at Lancaster that I was black?

**KENNEY**  No.

**SARAH**  Really?

*(Beat.)*

**KENNEY**  Well, we did. But of course, you weren't, and of course, we knew you weren't when we hired you. So don't let it bother you. *(SARAH laughs.)* What?

**SARAH**  Nothing. So how many people did you fly in for interviews?

**KENNEY**  Three, including you.

**SARAH**  What was wrong with the other person?

**KENNEY**  Nothing. We really shouldn't be talking about this.

**SARAH**  Did I ask for less?

**KENNEY**  Sarah! This really isn't appropriate. You know? I never should have brought it up.

**SARAH**  I brought it up.

**KENNEY**  That's right. You never should have brought it up. *(Beat.)* So have you gotten those handwriting samples to the FBI?

**SARAH**  I'm working on it.

**KENNEY**  Good, I want to get this over with. *(She gives an awkward laugh.)* I mean, the whole thing is giving me a headache.

*Sarah's office, the next day.* PATRICK CHIBAS *stands before Sarah's desk. He holds a copy of the student newspaper. He is waiting impatiently.* SARAH *enters with* MEYERS.

**SARAH** *(Seeing* PATRICK*)* Hi, Patrick, hang on a minute. *(She crosses to her desk and pulls out a manila envelope.)* I did what they said and made a key, so the samples are just numbered and the key shows whose handwriting it is.

**MEYERS** Okay.

**SARAH** And do they know when . . . ?

**MEYERS** Couple of weeks? I don't know.

**SARAH** Okay, thanks. *(*MEYERS *leaves, closing the door behind him. To* PATRICK*)* Sorry about the wait. Did you get a letter from financial aid? I cleared up your scholarship. *(Pause.* PATRICK *studies her.)* Your father should be happy.

**PATRICK** You wanted to talk to me about my editorial, didn't you?

**SARAH** That was . . . yes.

**PATRICK** Am I not allowed to express my opinions now? Is that it?

**SARAH** No. That's not it. You just raised some . . . serious allegations and I thought we should discuss them.

**PATRICK** So you can tell me I'm wrong.

**SARAH** No. I think you're right. Even though I think some of this is about me, probably. *(Beat.)* It is about me, isn't it?

**PATRICK**  Part of it, I guess. I mean, obviously most of it is about Dean Strauss.

**SARAH**  But this part . . . *(She picks up her own copy of the paper and reads)* "The discriminatory attitude of the administration, however, is not isolated to Dean Strauss and his outburst at Tuesday night's race forum. It is pandemic, as many students have come to learn the hard way. One student tells of being called upon in his sociology class to give the 'African American point of view.' Another tells of being offered a minority scholarship before the college even knew his race or ethnicity, as if any minority would do. This treatment reeks of tokenism and is an insult to the achievements of all students of color at Belmont."

*(Beat.)*

**PATRICK**  I didn't mention you by name.

**SARAH**  I appreciate that, I guess.

**PATRICK**  Do you want to know why?

**SARAH**  No.

**PATRICK**  It's because I sat here and took it from you. Twice. For twelve thousand dollars.

**SARAH**  No, you didn't. You let me know you were angry. Not Hispanic. Nuyorican.

**PATRICK**  Not Nuyorican. Puerto Rican. But I've never even been to Puerto Rico.

**SARAH**  I'm sorry, Patrick. I really wanted to do right by you. It was important to me to see that you got that scholarship.

**PATRICK**  See, if you could just admit that what you did was wrong—

**SARAH**  I know it was wrong. I realized that. *(Beat.)* But you got the scholarship.

**PATRICK**  But why does it have to come at a price? Why is there always some price?

**SARAH**  I thought . . . I was working hard to make the college pay you something so that . . . I wanted the price to be in their debit column. Do you see?

**PATRICK**  No.

**SARAH**  See, I used to work for this very poor, inner-city college with no money for anybody and I couldn't give anybody scholarships, and when I got here and saw what I could do, you know, how much money there was and how I could just fix some things, like the fraternities, you know . . . how I made them coed?

**PATRICK**  I'm not in a fraternity.

**SARAH**  I know you're not. I just thought I could make amends somehow, in a tangible way. If I just cut through all the rigmarole and if I was just up front about what I was doing, and . . . I just . . . I don't know. Am I making any sense?

**PATRICK**  No.

**SARAH**  I just wanted you to get the scholarship. I thought you'd, you know, take it and go on to solve the red tide or something.

**PATRICK**  The red tide?

**SARAH**  Or something. *(She tries to laugh.* PATRICK *stares at her.)* But I guess I was wrong. I wasn't paying attention to the details of your composition.

**PATRICK**  What does that mean? "The details of my composition." What does that mean?

SARAH  I wasn't paying attention to who you are.

PATRICK  No shit.

*(Pause.* SARAH *looks a little sickened.)*

SARAH  You know, Patrick, I'm afraid it's a hazard of the
job . . . Sometimes I slip into a certain way of speaking, or
relating to people— *(Laughs.)* Like that. "Relating to
people." You know? I don't normally talk like that, but so
many people come in and you talk to so many students . . .
*(She trails off.)* So I guess I'm saying that, without realizing
it, even in spite of your best intentions, sometimes you
start to talk to people like you're a bank clerk.

PATRICK  I don't think this is my problem. Whatever it is
you're talking about.

SARAH  I'm just trying to explain.

PATRICK  Look, here's why I agreed to come and talk to you.
I'm applying to NYU for the spring. Okay? I'm not staying
here.

SARAH  Patrick.

PATRICK  I hate this place. You know? You can give me twelve
thousand dollars and I don't care. It's not worth it. My
father says if I stay here, all I'll learn is shame.

SARAH  That's not all you'll learn.

PATRICK  *(Overriding her)* Also, I should tell you that I sent a
copy of the editorial to President Garvey and to the board
of advisers, or whatever, along with a letter telling them I'm
transferring and saying that this is pretty much why.

SARAH  I wish you would just take some time. I know you're
angry, but I wish you'd take some time and reconsider.

PATRICK  I hate Vermont. Also, all the kids in the Black Student Union and me and everybody I know, practically, are boycotting the next race forum, so you can tell Dean Strauss that he can yell as much as he wants but we won't be there to listen to him. *(He starts to leave.)*

SARAH  Patrick! . . .

PATRICK  *(Stops.)* What.

*(Beat.)*

SARAH  I feel like I've failed you.

PATRICK  Well . . . I don't know what to tell you except, you shouldn't have said those things to me.

SARAH  I'm sorry.

PATRICK  I don't know, Dean Daniels. You just keep apologizing all the time, like you want me to pass my hand over your head and make it all better. You know? Like I'm a saint, or something.

SARAH  I don't, really.

PATRICK  I'm not a saint.

SARAH  No. You're just a kid.

PATRICK  I'm not a kid, either. I mean, I'm right here in front of you. Are you even looking at me?

SARAH  I am. And I see a very smart young man who—

PATRICK  *(Overlapping, starting to leave)* Forget it.

SARAH  Who should reconsider because it's ridiculous to let your talent go to waste—

PATRICK  *(Interrupting)* I don't want to reconsider and I don't want any more compliments! I'm not some genius or something. I'm just whatever I am and I want to go someplace where I won't stand out. *(Opening the door)*

SARAH  Patrick—!

PATRICK  No, that's all you have to know. I don't want to discuss it, I don't want to be picked at, I just want to go. *(He leaves, slamming the door behind him.)*

SARAH  *(Almost to herself)* Patrick. *(Beat.)* I'm sorry.

# act two

*Sarah's office, a few hours later. It is nighttime.*

ROSS  You know, I grew up on a farm. I had a rural experience. But now I'm very much a part of the institution, so how could I call myself an outsider?

SARAH  I don't know.

ROSS  Me neither. But Foster's argument is that any expression that challenges the "establishment"—and that's actually the word he used, the "establishment"—whether it originates from a formally trained artist or not, constitutes "outsider" art. So by his definition, I could make outsider art.

SARAH  I don't even know what outsider art is.

ROSS  Well, it's just a fancy term for folk art.

SARAH  So what's wrong with saying folk art?

ROSS  I guess people thought it was diminutive.

SARAH  How?

ROSS  Well, to be a folk artist is to be untrained, which usually entails being disadvantaged. Economically, I mean. And undereducated.

SARAH  Or uneducated.

ROSS  "Undereducated," I guess, is the preferred term.

SARAH  So it's just art made by poor stupid people.

ROSS  I wouldn't put it that way.

SARAH  So my family could make outsider art. If any of them wanted to change hobbies and give up drinking.

*(Beat.)*

**ROSS** Are you okay?

**SARAH** I don't know. Lately, I look around here and I feel like I don't live up to the architecture. All the granite. The white columns. The blue shutters and slate roofs. It's all so . . . college-y.

**ROSS** I like Belmont. I've always thought it was very pleasing to the eye.

**SARAH** But doesn't it ever make you feel ugly?

**ROSS** Ugly how?

**SARAH** Like being ugly, like saying ugly things? Sometimes I want to run out onto the quad and hike up my skirt and pee all over everything.

**ROSS** See, I think that you're so conditioned to repressing your feelings that natural anger or frustration gets suppressed until you can't help but express it in some inappropriate way. If you were a painter you could be a Jackson Pollock and let your rage fly out onto the canvas, but you're not, you're a . . .

**SARAH** Administrator.

**ROSS** Administrator and so you . . .

**SARAH** Pee all over the grass.

**ROSS** Right.

**SARAH** But I'm also a person, too. You know? I'm not an object. To be studied. I'm not the subject of a painting. I'm not here to be aestheticized.

**ROSS** Why do you say that?

**SARAH** Sometimes I think that's what you do. You make everyone the subject of a lecture.

ROSS  I do not.

SARAH  Yes, you do.

ROSS  No, I don't.

SARAH  *(Quoting)* "There was this man on the train and his shirt cuffs were frayed and his shoe leather was cracked and he held this card before him like a beacon . . ."

*(Beat.)*

ROSS  What is your point?

SARAH  I don't think poverty is romantic.

ROSS  I wasn't romanticizing him. I was trying to understand him.

SARAH  You were idealizing him.

ROSS  Because I thought he seemed strong?

SARAH  Yes.

ROSS  But he was so neatly dressed, and so focused. He seemed strong. What's wrong with that?

SARAH  You idealized him and that means that you didn't respect him.

ROSS  What?

SARAH  To idealize is to fundamentally mark as different; it is not to respect. It is to fundamentally mark as different and, therefore, not equal. So that man on the train could never be your equal.

ROSS  Sure he could.

SARAH  No, he couldn't.

ROSS  You can't assume that. He may be my equal. I don't know. I don't know him. If I got to know him, then maybe we could find that out.

**SARAH** No, there's no objective measurement of whether or not he's your equal. That's not my point. I'm saying that you're not *allowing* him to be your equal.

**ROSS** I might if I knew him.

**SARAH** But you'll never get to know him. He's a poor crazy man. You'll always just stare at him on the train. You idealize him or you denigrate him, but either way you see him as fundamentally different. He is not your equal, you cannot respect him.

**ROSS** I can.

**SARAH** No, you can't.

**ROSS** I can.

**SARAH** No, you can't.

**ROSS** Why are you insisting on this?

**SARAH** It's important.

**ROSS** To you?

**SARAH** Yes. *(Beat.)* I screwed up this kid's scholarship.

**ROSS** What?

**SARAH** I screwed up this kid's scholarship. I thought if I was up front about it, then it wouldn't be wrong, because I thought maybe we were in on it together, but of course the balance of power was off and so he wasn't "in on" anything. You know? But I thought that he was a genius, and that he would solve the red tide and save the manatees. But I didn't know the first thing about him, and I screwed it up.

**ROSS** I didn't understand anything you just said.

**SARAH** I . . . Nothing. *(Beat.)* To idealize is not to respect. *(Beat.)* Why aren't you home with Petra?

**ROSS** She has a rehearsal tonight.

SARAH  For the fall dance recital.

ROSS  Right. Are you going?

SARAH  No. I just approved the funds for the posters. I don't really like dance. Everybody all "in tune" with their bodies. I think the whole mind/body dichotomy should be given another chance.

*(Beat.)*

ROSS  I don't know, Sarah. Sometimes I think you focus on the negative aspects of every situation. You're very cynical.

SARAH  Great.

ROSS  What?

SARAH  It's just a constant refrain. Sooner or later everybody tells me I'm cynical.

ROSS  How do you respond?

SARAH  I don't think I'm cynical. I think I'm honest.

ROSS  But you're not.

SARAH  What do you mean?

ROSS  You're withholding something.

SARAH  I am?

ROSS  Keeping something in reserve.

SARAH  Why do you say that?

ROSS  I don't know. I just feel it. *(Beat.)* You're equivocating.


## Scene two


*Sarah's office, a few days later:* SARAH *isn't there, but* STRAUSS *is sitting in the office anyway, reading a typewritten manuscript.* KENNEY *walks in briskly.*

**KENNEY**  Where is she?

**STRAUSS**  I don't know.

**KENNEY**  What are you doing here?

**STRAUSS**  You were right, Catherine. I did need to compose.
*(He hands her the manuscript.)* My *mea culpa.*

**KENNEY**  What?

**STRAUSS**  They were right. I've assimilated.

**KENNEY**  Assimilated?

**STRAUSS**  Adopted the attributes of the cultural elite in order
to succeed in a world that was not my own. It was Sarah
who made me realize it. She said I had an Old World
manner.

*(Beat.)*

**KENNEY**  You went to Groton.

**STRAUSS**  Precisely. *(SARAH enters, carrying a take-out bag.)*
Sarah, I've come to thank you.

**SARAH**  You have?

**STRAUSS**  And to give you an advance copy of the talk I've
prepared for tonight's forum. Feel free to jot notes in the
margins.

**SARAH**  I might not have time to read it.

**STRAUSS**  Then keep it for your records. *(SARAH takes it.)*
What is that in the bag?

**SARAH**  My lunch.

**STRAUSS**  What is it?

**SARAH**  A tuna salad sandwich. *(Beat.)* And chips.

**STRAUSS**  On rye?

**SARAH**  On raisin bread, actually.

**STRAUSS**  Really? I've never tried it. Is it good?

SARAH  Yeah. You can get one at the cafeteria.

STRAUSS  Excellent, I'll try it. Catherine, good day.

(STRAUSS *exits. Beat.*)

SARAH  Was that his vulnerable side?

KENNEY  (*Ignoring her*) President Garvey called and he's gotten a letter from this Patrick Chibas student. Do you know about this?

SARAH  Yes.

KENNEY  President Garvey is very upset. He says all we're doing is sowing racial discord, not racial harmony, and what do we plan to do about it? (*Beat.*) So? What do we plan to do about it?

SARAH  I don't know.

KENNEY  Sarah.

SARAH  I don't. I'm sorry.

KENNEY  Well, you better come up with something, because that's why we hired you. So here's what I want. I want a ten-point plan with specific, concrete suggestions that don't involve a lot of funding but will have a great impact, and I want you to type it up so that any idiot can understand it. Type it up in a bulleted list.

SARAH  A bulleted list?

KENNEY  Yes. A list with bullets to the side.

SARAH  (*Overlapping*) I know what a bulleted list is.

KENNEY  Then what?

SARAH  You want me to solve racism with a bulleted list?

KENNEY  Yes.

SARAH  I can't.

KENNEY  Well, if you can't, then we don't need you, Sarah.

SARAH  I've never claimed to be an expert—

KENNEY  *(Overlapping)* Garvey is livid! The board is livid, and I can't blame them. This Patrick Chibas could go to the press!

SARAH  He won't.

KENNEY  We're already in the Boston papers. Are you aware of that?

SARAH  No.

KENNEY  "Racial incident at Belmont." "Racists run Belmont ragged."

SARAH  It didn't really say that, did it?

KENNEY  It was the gist! The gist! We never should have started all this goddamn dialogue. This was an internal affair until you called the police.

*(Beat.)*

SARAH  When do you want the list?

KENNEY  Tomorrow.

SARAH  Tomorrow? We've got a stupid forum tonight.

KENNEY  If you start whining, Sarah, I'll ask someone else to do it.

SARAH  I am not whining.

KENNEY  Fine.

SARAH  I—

*(There's a knock at the door.)*

KENNEY  You what?

*(MEYERS pokes his head in.)*

MEYERS  Sarah? *(Sees KENNEY.)* Oh, excuse me.

KENNEY  Come in, I have to go anyway. *(To SARAH)* I'll come by in the morning.

(KENNEY *exits.* MEYERS *closes the door behind her, then walks over to Sarah's desk and puts down a rock.)*

**SARAH**  What's this?

**MEYERS**  A rock.

**SARAH**  And?

**MEYERS**  Somebody threw it through Simon's window.

**SARAH**  Is he all right?

**MEYERS**  He's fine. Holding up.

**SARAH**  Did he see anything?

**MEYERS**  Came home from classes, there it was.

**SARAH**  Who is doing this?

**MEYERS**  I wish I knew. Anyway, you'll have to take it to the police.

**SARAH**  Me?

**MEYERS**  Everybody keeps touching everything and they can't get a decent set of prints. I'm tired of them yelling at me.

**SARAH**  *(Picks up the rock.)* Can they even get fingerprints from a rock?

**MEYERS**  See!

(SARAH *drops the rock.)*

**SARAH**  Sorry. *(Looks at it.)* I'm not taking it to the police. I don't want to get yelled at. I'm tired of getting yelled at, too.

**MEYERS**  You know, I came by earlier and you weren't here, and Dean Strauss was just sitting in here, staring at the air.

**SARAH**  He's very strange.

**MEYERS**  That wasn't it. I was just thinking, maybe you ought to lock your office when you go out. Speaking as a security guard.

SARAH  I don't even have a key.

MEYERS  You don't?

SARAH  They said I didn't need one, what with the honor code
and all.

MEYERS  *(Laughs.)* I'll get you a key. I'll have to get you a
lock to go with it, but I'll get you a key.

SARAH  I'd really appreciate that.

MEYERS  No problem. *(Beat.)* Listen, Simon asked me to ask
you not to tell his parents about this. About the rock. He
said they'd make him come home.

SARAH  They're very worried.

MEYERS  I bet.

SARAH  I can't really lie to them, though.

MEYERS  I'm not telling you what to do. I'm just passing that
along.

SARAH  I'll go talk to him. *(Small beat.)* Or no, better yet,
I'll call a campus-wide meeting and put it up for a
vote. *(Beat.* MEYERS *stares at her.)* Nobody laughs at my
jokes.

MEYERS  That was a joke?

SARAH  Yes!

MEYERS  Sorry. It's hard to tell these days.


## Scene three

*Sarah's office, much later that night.* SARAH *is working by the
light of a lamp. She is struggling with her bulleted list. There
is a knock at the door which startles her. She yells.*

**Rebecca Gilman**

**SARAH** Who is it?

**ROSS** *(From offstage)* Ross.

**SARAH** Come in.

*(*ROSS *enters.)*

**ROSS** What are you doing here so late?

**SARAH** What are *you* doing here so late?

**ROSS** I was taking a walk.

**SARAH** What's wrong?

**ROSS** Petra and I had a big fight.

**SARAH** So was I right? Was she mad at you for sleeping around?

**ROSS** I didn't sleep around. I slept with you.

**SARAH** But was she mad?

**ROSS** Yes.

**SARAH** Ha. Radicals.

**ROSS** Don't sneer.

**SARAH** Did you apologize?

**ROSS** Yes.

**SARAH** Did you follow your apology with "But we had an agreement."

**ROSS** *(Reluctantly)* Yes.

**SARAH** Maybe you should leave that out next time.

**ROSS** It doesn't matter. We always fight.

**SARAH** Because you're so passionate?

**ROSS** No. I used to think we were passionate. Now I just think we're incompatible. *(Small beat.)* I'm tired.

**SARAH** I'm sorry.

**ROSS** It's okay. It's my own fault. *(Changing the subject)* So what are you doing up here so late?

**SARAH**  Making a bulleted list.

**ROSS**  Of course. For what?

**SARAH**  Catherine wants a plan. She wants to know how we can fix the racial discord we've sown.

**ROSS**  *We've* sown? I love that. It's her complete lack of understanding. It's Burton's ridiculous posturing. That forum tonight was a laughingstock. That thing Burton read? Jesus. *(He laughs.)* Just because he didn't make the soccer team at Groton.

**SARAH**  At least nobody was there to hear it.

**ROSS**  It was rather sparsely attended, wasn't it.

**SARAH**  The Black Student Union was boycotting.

**ROSS**  They were?

**SARAH**  Didn't you notice that there were just a lot of white people there?

**ROSS**  Well, yes. But, I mean, even when everyone's there, there's still just a lot of white people. I didn't know we were being boycotted.

**SARAH**  Yes.

**ROSS**  I had no idea. *(Beat.)* Then maybe Catherine's right? We should make a list. A plan. That's what you suggested in the first place, wasn't it?

**SARAH**  Back when I thought I had a clue.

**ROSS**  So what have you got so far? *(SARAH hands him a list. He reads)* "One. Stop being stupid." Sarah. "Two. Move to Vermont." What does that mean?

**SARAH**  Just that, you know, if you don't like black people, moving to Vermont can take care of that. Because there aren't any black people here.

**Rebecca Gilman**

**ROSS** "Three. Admit defeat." Sarah. You shouldn't do things like this.

**SARAH** Why not?

**ROSS** Because it sounds terrible.

**SARAH** Well, I'm just being honest.

**ROSS** Which is what makes it so terrible. I really wonder about you sometimes.

**SARAH** I have moments, is all.

**ROSS** Moments of what?

**SARAH** Moments of despair.

**ROSS** Is that all?

**SARAH** Isn't that enough?

*(Beat.)*

**ROSS** That kid that you were telling me about, whose scholarship you screwed up, that was Patrick Chibas, wasn't it?

**SARAH** Yes.

**ROSS** He is one of my students. My survey class. That's why I didn't recognize him. He came and told me he's transferring today. NYU.

**SARAH** Yeah.

**ROSS** I read his editorial. I . . . I just didn't put it together. I guess I was really focusing in on all the nasty things he had to say about Burton.

**SARAH** Yeah.

**ROSS** So you thought he would do something with the red tide?

**SARAH** I thought I would help him. The way I used to think I would help people. *(Beat.)* I don't know what I was thinking. I've really regressed.

**ross** How's that?

**sarah** I . . . When I went to graduate school, I really wanted to go into administration, because I had this misguided desire to help people.

**ross** Misguided how?

**sarah** You know, like a missionary or something.

**ross** Is that what you were doing with Patrick?

**sarah** I don't know. I didn't think I was. I thought I was just being up front. Pragmatic. You know? I thought pragmatism was a potential cure. Like, maybe I couldn't have the right attitude, but at least I could give twelve thousand dollars to somebody who needed it. But I couldn't even do that right.

**ross** What do you mean, the right attitude?

**sarah** Well . . . you know.

**ross** No, I don't.

**sarah** Just the racial thing.

**ross** What racial thing?

**sarah** That thing. You know. The thing. Where you do the whole thing and then you have the right attitude.

**ross** What whole thing?

**sarah** The moment of realization. The guilt. The transformation. (ross *looks to her for an explanation.*) The thing where you think you're not racist and then you learn how you are racist. And then you stop being racist. (*He waits.*) Like, maybe you think you're really liberal, so you decide to go into some field where you can help minority students. So you go to graduate school. But when you get there, you meet people who are a lot smarter than you, and also a lot more abrasive than you, and they point out that your desire to help minority students doesn't have anything to do with a sense of justice or fair play. Instead, it stems from your "plantation mentality." Your paternalism. Your desire to help the noble savage.

ROSS  You actually thought about it in those terms?

SARAH  Not consciously, no. But that's what I learned. I learned that I was thinking in those terms. When I got to graduate school. From those people. Who were so much smarter than me.

ROSS  So you were enlightened?

SARAH  That's what I was aiming for. Enlightenment. Definitely. I went to seminars in the education department. I took every class on African American literature and theory I could find. I read all this stuff I'd never read before. The whole shebang from Frederick Douglass to Henry Louis Gates, Jr., to bell hooks. I wanted to hear the African American voice and the African American viewpoint. And I listened and I absorbed, because I was scared shitless to actually say anything. Because what I learned real fast was that I was the one. It was me. I was the one who had kept black people down. Or if not me, personally, then I was still responsible by proxy.

ROSS  Are you being sarcastic?

SARAH  No, I really, I felt . . . I felt terrible. Everything I read indicted me. I wanted to apologize to the entire race and empty my pockets and say, "Here! Take it! Take it! What's mine is yours! Take it! I'm sorry! I'm so so sorry!" Hell, by the time we read *Native Son* I was so worked up I was convinced somebody was going to kill me in my bed and chop me up and shove me in a furnace, but I didn't care, because I deserved it. I was Mary Dalton. I was the stupid white girl. "Chop me up! Shove me in a furnace and when you sift through the ashes and find my bones wear them on a chain around your neck and dance the dance of the righteous for you are good and I am bad!"

ROSS  Maybe you were missing the point . . .

SARAH  No. I got the point. I just still thought it was all about me, you see. I cherished how badly I felt. I had been a racist. And I had repented.

ROSS  You shouldn't be so hard on yourself. Maybe some of your motivations were selfish, but you confronted the worst in yourself.

SARAH  No. It was a false conversion. *(Beat.)* You see, I'm afraid I'm going to start the whole thing over again.

ROSS  What thing?

SARAH  The thing that happened at Lancaster. What if it happens here, with Hispanics. Or Nuyoricans. Or whatever.

ROSS  What do you mean?

SARAH  I came here to get away from Lancaster. *(Beat.)* Because I hated Lancaster.

ROSS  What?

SARAH  It made me worse. *(Small beat.)* I mean, before I started there, I was just paternalistic. Now I'm fully aware that black people have agency and are responsible and can help themselves, but I think they don't do it because they're lazy and stupid.

ROSS  Sarah!

SARAH  So back then, when I thought I had learned my lesson,

I hadn't. I haven't. All I learned was how to appreciate black people. The way you might appreciate a painting or a good bottle of Bordeaux. I studied them to figure them out. Like Sanskrit. But that's no different than hating them.

ROSS  Oh, for godsake.

SARAH  It's not.

ROSS  It is!

SARAH  It's called objectification, Ross. And it relies on keeping the object of your investigation at bay. It relies on knowing one or two really well-educated black people. Because when you come face-to-face with a lot of just regular black people, you can't aestheticize them anymore. They're too damn scary.

ROSS  Jesus, Sarah.

SARAH  Look, this is . . . I've been struggling with this for a long, long time. I have. I thought I was fine, I thought I was making progress, until I got that job at Lancaster. I thought I was fine. But then I had to move to Chicago, and I don't know. Everything seemed different. All my newfound self-awareness and societal insight and . . . and all that crap, all that crap just flew out the window. So quickly. Because in the abstract, black people were fine. But in reality, they were so rude. And it wasn't my first exposure, you know, to a black population. I'd lived in a big city before. But my relationship with them was different this time. They weren't serving me anymore. I was serving them.

ROSS  At Lancaster?

SARAH  Yes. I shouldn't have been there and I knew I shouldn't have been there and I occasionally apologized for being there. But I still thought I could do a good job. And then I met the students. *(Beat.)* And they were all black. Of course. And some of them were great, and some of them were okay, and some of them were pains in the ass, and some of them were awful. Which is how the world is, except that the ones who were awful seemed really, exceptionally awful. They were loud and belligerent and abusive, and they walked down the hall in packs and they were so loud, and I couldn't understand a word they were saying, and they would glare at me, and if I didn't get out of their way, they ran me over. They pushed me aside.

ROSS  The way they've been pushed aside all their lives.

SARAH  So I tried to tell myself. Now I know how it feels, I said. But you know what? That worked for about a minute. And then I just got pissed off. They were so rude and loud and stupid.

ROSS  All of them?

SARAH  No. There were plenty of nice kids, but they weren't the ones you noticed. You noticed the awful ones, because they dominated the landscape. *(Beat.)*

And I was living in Chicago and I was taking the train to work and it was the same thing on the train. There'd be a dozen black people sitting quietly, going about their business, but there'd be two incredibly loud, stinky, offensive black guys at one end of the car and they'd be the ones I'd notice. And I'd tell myself not to pay attention to them. That they weren't representative of their entire race. I knew that. I kept telling myself I just had to get used to them. It was just a matter of learning. *(Beat.)*

**Rebecca Gilman**

But then I noticed that I'd started slipping into a pattern when I got on the train. First I'd look for an empty seat next to a white woman. And then a white man. And then a black woman, and then, last choice, a black man. And sometimes, if the only empty seats were next to black men and if they were wearing big puffy coats, then I would just stand. *(Beat.)*

And then I started adding categories. White men, then Hispanic men, then Middle Eastern men—no, Asian men—*then* Middle Eastern men, and finally, always last, black men. Then I started qualifying things. If the black women had kids, then they came after some of the men, because the kids were a pain in the ass. Their mothers didn't watch them and they'd fall down and cry and then their mothers would yell at them for falling down. They'd yell, "That's what you get for standing up in the seat." *(Beat.)* "That's what you get." *(Small beat.)*

I felt bad about it at first. I'd get on the train and I'd wonder, What must that poor black man think, I'm so obviously avoiding him. He's a perfectly nice person. Sitting there. I see his face. He's a perfectly nice person. But I didn't want to take a chance. And, after a while, it sort of slipped my mind to feel bad about it. And then everything sort of slipped my mind. So that when I found myself sitting across from my students and thinking that they were scary, or that their hair was stupid, or that it was no wonder they were pregnant, I noticed, I guess, but I didn't care. I just felt tired, contemptuous. They weren't going to listen to me. They weren't going to graduate from college. They weren't going to do anything with their lives. Not because they couldn't, but because they didn't want to. Because they were lazy and stupid.

ROSS No, they weren't. They were poor. They were high-risk students—

SARAH I know all that, I know, I know. I knew that then. I know it now. And I never said anything . . . anything untoward. I was scrupulous. But I still looked at them and thought that they were stupid.

ROSS But you were encountering them after years and years of privation and discrimination. After an economic and educational system had utterly failed them.

SARAH Whatever.

ROSS You didn't care?

SARAH I guess I did, I just . . . It was so hard to care because they were so rude.

ROSS But they weren't all rude. You said yourself they weren't all rude.

SARAH No. But it's like I said: The only ones I noticed were the ones who were yelling.

ROSS So you were aware of this?

SARAH Yes. I was fully aware. Aware of the forces that shaped me, that shaped them, and yet unable to stop thinking that if they just wanted to, they could stop being so stupid.

ROSS So what happened? Please tell me that you . . . that you went to a priest and confessed and were absolved or something. Tell me something.

**Rebecca Gilman**

SARAH  No. I didn't. I just went to work and kept quiet about it. I guess I kept hoping it would go away. But then, it was like I had a viral infection that would flare up at the worst possible moments, and I started saying these . . . things.

ROSS  What sort of things?

SARAH  Well, this once, I was at the faculty Christmas party and I got drunk, and I told this English professor how much I hate Toni Morrison.

ROSS  You hate Toni Morrison?

SARAH  Yes.

ROSS  Why?

SARAH  Her books suck.

ROSS  That is so stupid.

SARAH  They do, though. *Beloved* sucked. Stylistically it's a mess. It's like a sloppy first draft. Third person, first person. Realism, magical realism. What the fuck?

ROSS  You're imposing traditional standards for a narrative structure on it that don't allow—

SARAH  Yeah, yeah, Eurocentric, patriarchal standards, and she's resisting and I'm saying rewrite. I know why I'm supposed to like her, but I don't. And I don't think that hating Toni Morrison makes you a racist. I just know that other people think it makes you a racist.

(Beat.)

ROSS  What's your point exactly?

SARAH  My point is that I didn't need to tell that professor that I don't like Toni Morrison, but I needed to tell him something. What I really wanted to do was unburden myself completely. To get it out of my system somehow.

*(Beat.* ROSS *regards her.)*

**ROSS** So you still feel this way?

**SARAH** Yes. It's just maybe not as bad, because there are hardly any black people here.

**ROSS** You moved to Vermont.

**SARAH** Yeah.

**ROSS** You ran away.

**SARAH** I didn't know what else to do. I was afraid of the kind of thoughts that popped into my head. I was afraid of what I might say. I began to fear for my soul. *(Small beat.)* Belmont, Vermont. Beautiful mountain, green mountain. I knew it would be quiet and clean and white. It wasn't a noble way to save myself, or a brave way, but it was the only way I could think of. *(Beat.)* But now I'm back where I started.

**ROSS** But you're not a dog.

**SARAH** Of course I'm not.

**ROSS** So you can help being a racist. You act like you can't, like a dog can't help chewing up the furniture, but you're not a dog, you're a human with a human-sized brain that works very well and that understands the dynamics of racism, and yet here you stand, a racist. It's almost like you're proud of it.

**SARAH** I'm not proud. I'm at a loss. I don't know what to do. That's my whole point. I say to myself over and over and over again, "Just stop it! You know you're doing it, just stop it!" and I still do it anyway. And it doesn't help that when I

try and articulate what's going on in my head, in even the
mildest way, I'm attacked.

ROSS  What do you want people to do? Congratulate you?

SARAH  No. But couldn't they listen to me? Or talk to me?
Couldn't they admit that, on occasion, even they feel the
same way?

ROSS  So you're suggesting what?

SARAH  *(Shrugs.)* Stop being stupid. Admit defeat.

ROSS  Don't back away. You're suggesting a real dialogue.

SARAH  Ideally, sure, but it's impossible.

ROSS  That's not true.

SARAH  Public dialogue is never real dialogue. Nobody will
admit to anything in a crowd. I mean, I can't believe
that I'm the only person that feels this way.

ROSS  All right. I'll admit something. I've never been able to
look at an African American without noting that he or she
is such.

SARAH  You mean, when you look at a black person you think,
There's a black person.

ROSS  Yes.

SARAH  Oooh. That's ugly.

ROSS  Well—

SARAH  That's pathetic! That's the most you can admit?

ROSS  I'm just playing along, Sarah. I want to understand your
point.

SARAH  Oh. Even better.

ROSS  All right! Let's say I'm secretly the grand hooba of the
KKK. Okay? Now what? Where do we go from here?

SARAH  *(Hesitates.)* I don't know.

**ROSS**  Well, you can't just criticize and criticize and never offer a solution.

**SARAH**  If I had a solution I'd put it in a goddamned bulleted list!

*(Beat.)*

**ROSS**  You're a terrible coward. Even if you can't find the perfect solution, you should find the best you can and at least give it a try.

**SARAH**  You mean, like, have a forum?

**ROSS**  Okay, it was a bad idea, but at least I tried. You have to go out on a limb, otherwise the best lack all conviction.

**SARAH**  What?

**ROSS**  Yeats. "The best lack all conviction, while the worst are full of passionate intensity."

**SARAH**  "The best lack all conviction."

**ROSS**  The worst are full of passionate intensity.

*(Beat.)*

**SARAH**  And I'm which?

**ROSS**  Neither. Right now, you're just awful. *(Pause.)* Look, I'm sorry. I mean, obviously you've struggled with this. You're struggling with this now, I can tell. But I don't think that just because you've struggled, you should be let off the hook. I think Catherine's right. I think you should come up with a plan.

**SARAH**  I don't know.

**ROSS**  You've got ideas already.

**SARAH**  I don't have anything.

**ROSS**  What about that recruiting program you were telling me about? The thing you did at Lancaster. That was a nice idea.

**SARAH** It didn't work.

**ROSS** It completely failed?

**SARAH** Well, there was about a forty percent success rate. *(Beat.)* So far.

**ROSS** See, Sarah, for all your professed resignation, I think that inherent in what you're saying is hope.

**SARAH** What do you mean?

**ROSS** Most people are just racists. They don't know they're racists. *(Beat.)* I know you have some good ideas.

**SARAH** I'm not so sure.

**ROSS** Don't put up barriers to this. I trust you. I trust you can do this.

**SARAH** Really?

**ROSS** Yes.

*(Beat.)*

**SARAH** Okay.

**ROSS** Does that mean you'll try?

*(Beat.)*

**SARAH** Yeah. Leave me alone. *(ROSS starts to go.)* Hey. Thanks for being so nice to me.

**ROSS** I wasn't being nice. *(Beat. This is very hard for him.)* That thing with the train? Choosing the seats? I do that, too.

**SARAH** Everybody does.

**ROSS** That doesn't make it right.

**SARAH** I know. *(Beat.)* I know, I know, I know.

# Scene four

*Sarah's office, the following morning.* SARAH *has fallen asleep at her desk.* MEYERS *enters, holding a piece of paper.*

**MEYERS**  Sarah?

**SARAH**  What?! . . . Oh God. I fell asleep.

**MEYERS**  I thought you should see this. *(Hands her the paper. She reads.)*

**SARAH**  Oh God.

**MEYERS**  Do you want me to go with you?

**SARAH**  I . . . Maybe I should go by myself.

**MEYERS**  Whatever you think's best. I'll walk you as far as my office.

**SARAH**  Thanks.

*(They exit, closing the door behind them. The chapel bells begin to chime their quarter-hour tune. The door opens again and* KENNEY *enters. She looks around, then goes to Sarah's desk and picks up the phone and dials.)*

**KENNEY**  President Garvey, please, Marion. *(Beat. She begins looking through Sarah's papers as she waits.)* He isn't? Are you sure? *(Beat.)* Fine. *(She hangs up. She is holding the legal pad. She reads. There are several used pages folded over the back of the pad and she flips them over and reads from the beginning. She doesn't look pleased. She takes the legal pad and leaves.)*

# Scene five

*Sarah's office a couple of hours later.* GREG SULLIVAN *is waiting for her.* SARAH *enters quickly. She isn't happy to see him.*

GREG  Hi, Dean Daniels! They said I could wait.

SARAH  Yes?

GREG  Greg Sullivan? Students for Tolerance?

SARAH  And?

GREG  I wondered, could we talk? We've got a bit of a problem with the group. Well, not with the group per se, but with Dean Strauss. We couldn't get him to stop talking. And the whole point of the group, if you remember, was to have a place where we could talk, the students, that is. Where we could have meaningful discussions.

SARAH  I thought the whole point was to get you into law school.

*(Beat.* GREG *is taken aback, but then he laughs.)*

GREG  Okay. That's fair. That's fair. That might have been a factor for me at first. But I'm seriously committed to this group now, and well, we're in sort of a bind.

SARAH  I'm in sort of a bind, too, right now, and I wonder if we could discuss this later.

GREG  Oh gosh. I just barged in, didn't I? Should I make an appointment?

SARAH  That would be good. *(She perfunctorily picks up her appointment book.)* Tomorrow at one?

GREG  Terrific. Thanks so much.

SARAH  Sure.

GREG  Bye.

*(He leaves. SARAH closes the door behind him, then goes to her desk and picks up the phone. Right away, though, she sees that the legal pad is missing. She hangs up the phone and starts looking for it.)*

SARAH  Shit. *(She picks up the phone again and dials. Into phone)* Did you come take my list? *(Beat.)* I need to talk to you . . . Ross, please . . . Okay. Thanks.

*(She hangs up. There's a knock on the door. SARAH looks around, then ducks underneath her desk, hiding. The door opens and KENNEY sticks her head in.)*

KENNEY  Sarah?

*(KENNEY hurries toward the desk and, without seeing SARAH, quickly puts the legal pad back where it was, trying to make it look as if nothing has been disturbed. She quickly leaves. SARAH cautiously emerges, studies the legal pad. A knock on the door. She ducks back under the desk. The door opens and ROSS enters.)*

ROSS  Sarah?

*(SARAH emerges again, banging her head.)*

SARAH  Ow.

ROSS  What are you doing?

SARAH  Picking up a . . . Hiding. Close the door. *(ROSS does.)* She had it.

ROSS  Who?

SARAH  Catherine. She came in here and took it, and then she brought it back and left it here for me. It's a trap.

ROSS  What?

SARAH  My list. I'm going to get fired.

**ROSS** Just because she saw your list? Let me see. *(SARAH hands him the pad.)* These are good suggestions. I've always wanted a cultural studies program—

**SARAH** Not that crap! Look back! Before that.

**ROSS** *(Flips back a few pages, reads.)* Sarah. I thought you got rid of all this. *(Sees something.)* What is this?

**SARAH** The pros and cons of living near black people versus living away from them.

**ROSS** *(Reads)* "Away: not scary. You forget about their hair." What were you doing?

**SARAH** I just . . . you know, I had to get it all out.

**ROSS** Why did you ever leave this where somebody could find it?

**SARAH** I had to go. I had to go talk to Simon. Ross. He was doing it to himself.

**ROSS** What?

**SARAH** He . . . The FBI, they sent us the results. *(She pulls a folded piece of paper out of her pocket.)* The handwriting was his. He was doing it to himself. *(ROSS stares at her.)* I went to his room, and I asked him. I said, "Simon? Did you do this?" And he just nodded and sat down on his bed and he started crying. He just kept crying and crying.

**ROSS** Why?

**SARAH** He doesn't know. He said it was like somebody else was doing it. He said that he can remember watching his hand as he wrote. He can see his hands folding the paper. He can see his hands taping it to his door. He said he knew he'd get caught, but he did it anyway.

**ROSS** He can't explain it?

SARAH  No. He just said he was relieved it was finally over.

ROSS  The poor kid. All this time, he's just been waiting.

SARAH  He said he was sorry. *(Pause.)* I don't know what to do, Ross.

ROSS  About what?

SARAH  I kept looking at his hands. When Simon said that. I kept looking at his hands. We were sitting there on his bed and he was crying and we were both staring at his hands and there they were. Hands. Just hands. His hands and my hands. And his hands. And mine. Next to each other. Mine in my lap. His in his. I just kept looking and looking. My fingers. The backs of my hands. I just kept thinking, This is me. This is me. This is me. *(Beat.)* So I told Simon, I said, "This is you." I rubbed his hand. I said, "This is you." *(Beat.)* "Stop hating yourself." *(Breaking down)* They were . . . they were just these hands . . .

*(Beat.)*

ROSS  It's okay.

SARAH  No, it's not.

ROSS  Of course it's not. I just . . . I don't know. I can't tell you what to do, Sarah.

## Scene six

*Sarah's office, a couple of hours later.* KENNEY, STRAUSS, ROSS, MEYERS, *and* SARAH *are there.* MEYERS *sits quietly in a corner.*

Rebecca Gilman

KENNEY  Well, this changes everything.

STRAUSS  He has no explanation?

KENNEY  This certainly changes everything.

ROSS  What does it change, exactly?

KENNEY  Everything. This is quite a development. *(Laughs.)* He's clearly quite a study, isn't he? What was he thinking?

SARAH  He doesn't know.

KENNEY  He wasn't thinking at all, was he?

STRAUSS  It's a textbook case. Internalized racism. Is he dark-skinned?

SARAH  Compared to what?

STRAUSS  Light-skinned blacks. It's an issue apparently, either way. Jean Toomer, for example—

SARAH  Jean Toomer?

STRAUSS  One of the foremost writers of the Harlem Renaissance.

SARAH  I know who Jean Toomer is.

STRAUSS  Oh.

SARAH  What does he have to do with Simon?

STRAUSS  I was just trying to make a point.

SARAH  You don't know Simon.

STRAUSS  Well, I—

SARAH  I don't think you've ever spoken to him.

STRAUSS  No.

SARAH  So you don't know him.

STRAUSS  No. *(Beat.)* You know, I hardly think you're in a position to—

**KENNEY** *(Overriding him)* He must have desperately wanted attention.

**SARAH** He doesn't know what he wanted.

**STRAUSS** *(Realizing something)* Ha! I know why! It just hit me. Little Black Sambo. Isn't that how he referred to himself in the notes?

**ROSS** Yeah.

**STRAUSS** And what did Little Black Sambo do?

**KENNEY** Just tell us.

**STRAUSS** Well, Little Black Sambo had some beautiful new clothes and he was walking in the jungle, showing them off, when a tiger jumped out of the bush and threatened to eat him. So Little Black Sambo offered the tiger his new coat in exchange for his life, and the tiger agreed and took his coat. And then another tiger popped up, and so on and so on, until the tigers had taken all of his clothes. Little Black Sambo was going home naked and forlorn when he heard a terrible noise coming from the forest, and he peeped around a tree and saw all of the tigers wearing his clothes and arguing over which of them was the grandest tiger of all. They argued and argued until they got so angry that they took off the clothes and started chasing each other around a tree. Well, Little Black Sambo saw this and he walked up and calmly put his clothes back on, knowing that the tigers were too intent on each other to pay him any mind. The tigers just kept chasing each other, faster and faster around the tree. They began spinning and spinning until they were just a yellow blur, and they spun so fast, they spun themselves into butter. So Little Black Sambo got himself a spoon and scooped up the butter and put it on his pancakes and ate the tigers up. *(He laughs.)* Which is just what Simon Brick did to us. He got us all in a whirl over nothing.

SARAH It doesn't have anything to do with us.

ROSS And it wasn't nothing.

STRAUSS He's a little fox. A little con man.

SARAH Think of him.

STRAUSS He's probably bragging about it to his friends right now.

SARAH Imagine him for half a second. That is not why he did it.

STRAUSS Why, then?

SARAH I don't know.

STRAUSS You don't know? But you're so in touch with him.

SARAH I never claimed to be "in touch" with anybody.

STRAUSS Don't be so modest. Tell us about the black man. Illuminate us.

*(Pause.)*

SARAH *(To* KENNEY*)* You showed it to him, didn't you?

KENNEY What?

SARAH It's not enough that you came in here and took it and read it, you showed it to him, too, didn't you?

KENNEY *(Beat. Considers.)* It was in plain view. Lying on your desk.

SARAH You had no right to read it.

KENNEY It was in plain view. *(Beat.)* Would you like to explain?

SARAH No.

**ROSS** You know, whatever you've read, you did it by violating Sarah's privacy—

**KENNEY** You know about this?

**ROSS** If you'll let me finish, I think that you have seen something out of context, and that to judge Sarah by what you've seen is unfair.

**KENNEY** I'm asking her to explain it to me right now. She says there's no explanation.

**STRAUSS** Except the obvious one, which is that she's a racist.

**SARAH** There is an explanation, but I choose not to tell it to you.

**ROSS** Sarah has been doing some soul-searching—

**SARAH** I choose not to tell it to them! *(To* STRAUSS *and* KENNEY, *picking up the pad)* Just use what you know. Public transportation? Scary! Toni Morrison? I hate her! So what if she won the Nobel Prize? So did Pearl S. Buck! La la la. *(They stare at her.)* Satisfied?

**KENNEY** That really wasn't what I was looking for.

**STRAUSS** Really. That was weird.

**SARAH** *(Reaching in her drawer, handing* KENNEY *an envelope)* Here.

**KENNEY** What's this?

**SARAH** My letter of resignation.

**ROSS** When did you do that?

**SARAH** Just before the meeting. I didn't even proofread it. Ha!

**KENNEY** This is all wrong.

**ROSS** I agree. We should discuss this and give Sarah a chance to collect herself.

**KENNEY** I don't think we should discuss anything, I just don't think we should be handling this in public.

**SARAH** In public?

*(*KENNEY *motions toward* MEYERS *with her head.)*

**MEYERS** Don't worry, I don't know what you're talking about.

**KENNEY** Then I think I'll send you over to Simon's room. Since we'll want him off campus as soon as possible, I think I'll have you pack up his things and drive him home.

**MEYERS** Ma'am?

**SARAH** *(Overlapping)* Drive him home? Aren't you going to talk to him?

**KENNEY** Simon wrote the notes, which means he's been lying to us all along, which means he's violated the honor code. That's grounds for expulsion. And fraud.

**SARAH** Wait a minute. He feels terrible. Give him a chance to explain if he wants to.

**KENNEY** The quickest way to heal is to get on with things. I think everyone will feel much better when he's gone. Mr. Meyers? Why don't you go over and tell Simon that he's been asked to leave and help him pack his things.

**MEYERS** No, ma'am.

**KENNEY** Pardon?

**MEYERS** I'm not telling him that. I'll help him out with his things, because I like him, but I won't be the bearer of bad news.

**STRAUSS** Let me tell him.

**SARAH** No!

**STRAUSS** I want to meet him.

**SARAH** I'll do it.

**KENNEY** You've quit.

**SARAH** I don't want you near him!

**STRAUSS** How do we know you won't go in there and scream "I hate Toni Morrison!" at him?

**SARAH** Because. I have always been polite.

**STRAUSS** You haven't been polite to me.

**SARAH** That's because I hate you. You so totally suck.

**ROSS** *(Overlapping)* Let's not do this. Sarah?

**SARAH** No, I do. I hate him. *(To* STRAUSS*)* Neh neh neh, I hate you. Okay? That's out in the open. Okay?

**STRAUSS** It was hardly a secret.

**SARAH** You hate me, too, okay?

**STRAUSS** Whatever you say, dear.

**SARAH** I'm going to talk to Simon, though, and you're not going near him. Me! Not you.

**KENNEY** I think you're all riled up.

**SARAH** I'll be fine. Okay? *(Draws a breath.)* Look. I'm fine.

**KENNEY** I don't know.

**ROSS** I'll go with her.

*(As they leave)*

**KENNEY** Oh, fine. All three of you go, but, Sarah, if you say anything offensive . . .

**SARAH** You'll fire me? Ha ha ha. I quit!

*(*SARAH *fairly runs out.* ROSS *and* MEYERS *follow.)*

**STRAUSS** I can't believe you let her go.

**KENNEY** Well, I don't want to talk to him.

**STRAUSS** But I wanted to meet him.

**Rebecca Gilman**

**KENNEY**  You'd say something stupid without even knowing it and open us up to a lawsuit.

**STRAUSS**  I'm happy to know you think so well of me. You'd rather the crazy racist go talk to him.

**KENNEY**  Well, she hasn't actually done anything overt. She was doing a good job until all of this came up.

**STRAUSS**  But you never liked her.

**KENNEY**  No. I screwed up the job search. I had to hire her.

**STRAUSS**  It doesn't bother me that she hates me. I mean, she's obviously insane.

**KENNEY**  What a stupid waste of time.

**STRAUSS**  But I have to admit, there's still some part of me that flinches when I'm rejected, even if I'm rejected by someone I don't respect.

**KENNEY**  I wonder how long I should wait to call Simon's parents.

**STRAUSS**  You're not listening to me.

**KENNEY**  You've had your feelings hurt, but you're right: she's insane. She was obviously threatened by you and so she felt compelled to attack.

**STRAUSS**  Exactly. Thank you.

**KENNEY**  I want him to be well on his way home so that they can't protest or try to come up here and talk things out.

**STRAUSS**  What?

**KENNEY**  Simon Brick. I want to call his parents after he's left so there's no turning back.

**STRAUSS**  Oh. Well, how long is the drive? Six hours?

**KENNEY**  To Albany?

STRAUSS  I thought he was from Maryland somewhere.

KENNEY  I'm sure it's Albany.

STRAUSS  I don't know, then. I've never been to Albany.

KENNEY  Maybe I'll just let them call me. *(Beat.)* I feel sorry
for Simon. I'm afraid it will take him some time to recover
from this.

STRAUSS  He'll be fine.

KENNEY  I think he just wanted attention.

STRAUSS  No. He's a little con artist. *(Smiles.)* A crafty little
fox.


## Scene seven

*Sarah's office, the next day.* SARAH *is packing up boxes.* ROSS *is
talking to her.*


ROSS  It wasn't funny yesterday, when it was happening, of
course, but last night, when I was telling Petra about it, we
couldn't stop laughing. The look on Burton's face was just
priceless. *(He laughs, remembering.)* But you really did
handle yourself well with Simon yesterday. I was truly im-
pressed. I really think you've changed.

SARAH  No, I haven't.

ROSS  Yes, you have. You said so yourself. You had to look at
Simon and see him as an individual, and you saw how your
attitude was hurting him, and you knew that your racism
had become untenable. You had an epiphany.

SARAH  No, because I don't believe in shit like that. Ergo my previous, completely fraudulent "awakening." It didn't take. Because there are no transformational moments. You don't become a better person overnight.

ROSS  Then yesterday was a turning point.

SARAH  No.

ROSS  But you said yourself, you looked at his hands, you looked at yours.

SARAH  And what?

ROSS  Saw that you're no different.

SARAH  Saw that we're both human beings?

ROSS  Yes.

SARAH  Admitted Simon into the inner sanctum of *Homo sapiens*?

ROSS  Don't put it that way.

SARAH  I've always known he was human, you idiot.

ROSS  Then what?

SARAH  You're black, I thought. And I'm white.

ROSS  That's it?

SARAH  Yes.

ROSS  That was really it?

SARAH  That's all I thought.

*(Beat.)*

ROSS  Look, I have to go, I have a class. Can you meet me for a beer later? I still want to talk about this.

SARAH  No.

ROSS  Six o'clock?

SARAH  I said no.

ROSS  Should I come by here?

SARAH  Come by if you want, I won't be here.

**ROSS** Yes, you will. *(He exits.)*

**SARAH** *(Yelling)* Know-it-all! *(SARAH pauses, then turns back to a box and starts loading things into it, not really paying attention to what she's doing. MEYERS enters and knocks on her open door. She turns.)* Hi.

**MEYERS** Hi.

**SARAH** How'd it go?

**MEYERS** Okay.

**SARAH** He's home?

**MEYERS** Safe and sound.

*(Pause.)*

**SARAH** So. I'm leaving.

**MEYERS** I see that.

*(Pause.)*

**SARAH** What'd y'all talk about? On the way?

**MEYERS** Not a lot. Baseball. He thinks the Pirates might have a chance at something in a couple of years. They're a young team. They still have something to prove.

**SARAH** I see.

**MEYERS** He's too young to remember Roberto Clemente, but from what he knows about him, he thinks he was a great man.

**SARAH** That's nice.

**MEYERS** Yeah.

**SARAH** Were his parents home?

**MEYERS** No. He let himself in. I helped him carry his things. He offered me a Diet Coke. I didn't really want one, but I did ask to use the rest room.

**SARAH** What was the house like?

**Rebecca Gilman**

**MEYERS** Nothing special. Not too big, not too little. The bathroom was nice. I guess it was a guest bathroom. They had the liquid soap in the dispenser, though, so you could really wash your hands. Sometimes people put little special soaps in the guest bathroom. Little soaps shaped like roses or something. I never know if I'm supposed to use them or just look at them.

*(Beat.)*

**SARAH** Did he seem sad?

**MEYERS** Not really. We stopped at a Burger King. I hope that's okay. I bought him dinner.

**SARAH** That's fine.

**MEYERS** He has a hearty appetite.

**SARAH** Did he say anything?

**MEYERS** I didn't ask.

**SARAH** So he never . . .

**MEYERS** He did say that he maybe made a mistake, asking for his own room. He said it left him feeling kind of lonely.

**SARAH** He said that?

**MEYERS** He said he's shy to start with, so maybe he shouldn't of cut himself off from people like that.

**SARAH** He said he's shy?

**MEYERS** That's how he put it.

**SARAH** Anything else?

**MEYERS** Nope. Mostly we didn't say anything. I asked him, did he want me to stay until his parents got home. He said, nothing personal but he kind of felt like he was under arrest, so would I mind leaving? I said, "Not at all." *(Beat.)* When I got home last night, I woke my wife up and I told her what all had happened, and she said it seemed like a shame, such a nice kid like that, doing himself in. So to speak.

SARAH  It is a shame.

MEYERS  So where are you headed?

SARAH  I'm going back to Chicago.

MEYERS  Could you get your old job back?

SARAH  I don't think so.

MEYERS  Does this kind of look bad for you, then?

SARAH  It kind of does. But I don't know. I don't think I'm suited to this line of work.

MEYERS  Maybe not.

*(Beat.)*

SARAH  Well, thanks for all your help.

MEYERS  Yeah. I just wish it could of turned out different.

SARAH  Me too.

MEYERS  No. I guess, I mean, I wish *you* could of turned out different.

SARAH  Pardon?

MEYERS  I thought, when we started this, that you weren't like them. You didn't want to make speeches or stand up in front of everybody, you just wanted to get down to work. I thought you were different. But I guess you were just hiding out, huh?

SARAH  I'm not sure I understand.

MEYERS  I mean, I guess I was upset last night. At what happened to that kid. I guess I looked at him and I figured that he wouldn't of done that to himself if somebody hadn't made him feel bad. If somebody hadn't put the words in his head. You know? I mean, those notes, they were mean and terrible, and I don't think you see yourself like that, like he did in those notes, if somebody hasn't already seen you that way first. That's all.

**SARAH**  I . . . yes. *(Beat.)* I'm sorry if I disappointed you.

**MEYERS**  I guess I just liked that kid.

**SARAH**  I like Simon, too.

**MEYERS**  Then how can you think those things?

**SARAH**  I guess that's what I have to figure out.

**MEYERS**  That seems kind of easy.

**SARAH**  It does?

**MEYERS**  Yeah. I mean, one part of you must be lying to the other part.

**SARAH**  What?

**MEYERS**  Either you're not as good as you think you are or you're not as bad as you think you are.

**SARAH**  I really do like Simon.

**MEYERS**  That's promising.

**SARAH**  But the other part of me is not lying.

*(Long pause.)*

**MEYERS**  Well, I hope you figure it out.

**SARAH**  Me too.

*(GREG SULLIVAN enters.)*

**GREG**  Hi.

**SARAH**  Hi.

**MEYERS**  Hey, there.

**GREG**  I had an appointment? *(SARAH laughs.)* Is this a bad time?

**SARAH**  Well, Greg, I've sort of . . .

**MEYERS**  She quit.

**GREG**  Oh. My. I'm sorry. Or congratulations, maybe, I don't know.

**SARAH**  Let's go with congratulations.

**GREG**  Okay, then. Congratulations.

**SARAH**  Thank you.

**GREG**  Should I talk to someone else?

**SARAH**  This is about Dean Strauss?

**GREG**  Yes, ma'am.

**SARAH**  *(Smiles.)* Right. Then you know what? I can probably help you out.

**MEYERS**  I'll leave you two alone. *(Starts to exit.)*

**SARAH**  Wait. *(She offers her hand.)* Thanks for everything.

**MEYERS**  *(Shakes her hand.)* Good luck to you, then, Sarah. *(He exits, closing the door behind him.)*

**GREG**  So you're leaving?

**SARAH**  Yes.

**GREG**  On to greener pastures, I hope.

**SARAH**  I hope. *(Beat.)* So Burton wouldn't shut up?

**GREG**  Well, as I mentioned yesterday, the whole point of the group was to give the students a chance to talk to each other, one on one. And really, we were willing to give time to Dean Strauss, but then it just started to get ridiculous. We couldn't get a word in edgewise. So finally, I . . . well, I lied. I told him that we were going to cancel the next couple of meetings because of midterms, and that we wouldn't meet again until next week. But we did meet again. It was sort of silly, but we had a secret meeting in my room. And really, it went so much better without him there. We really started to talk about our feelings and our experiences with African Americans, or, to be more precise, our complete lack of experience, which was only compounded by the fact that there were still no black students in the group. (SARAH *laughs.*) Right. It was ridiculous. So I got an idea. When I heard that the Black Student Union was boycotting the forums, I gave Claudia Thompson a call. You know, their president?

SARAH  Yes, I know Claudia.

GREG  And I said, "Look, we've got this little group going, it's not much, but we're committed to opening up a real dialogue about race. The only problem is, we're all white."

SARAH  And what did she say to that?

GREG  She laughed, too. So I told her that we would love it if the BSU would come and join us at our next meeting. And when I told her that we were actually meeting in my room, you know, so we could avoid Dean Strauss, that convinced her that we were okay. So she offered the Union house and we met there last night.

SARAH  You did?

GREG  And it was terrific. People were really talking. There was yelling and screaming and people were even crying. I mean it. We all really got into it and people were saying things . . . things I'd never expect anybody to admit to. But it was all so open. You know? The spirit was right.

SARAH  The spirit?

GREG  Yes. The spirit was right. And so we all just opened up. And nobody's feelings were hurt, and afterward we had a huge group hug, and we're meeting again next week.

**SARAH**  How many people? In this group hug?

**GREG**  I'd say fifteen, total. *(SARAH smiles.)* What? You're not making fun, are you?

**SARAH**  No. I think it's great. So what's the problem?

**GREG**  Well, we obviously can't have Dean Strauss come back. It would ruin everything.

**SARAH**  Would you like me to find you another sponsor?

**GREG**  Well, the thing is, we were wondering, do we have to have a sponsor at all?

**SARAH**  *(Considers.)* No. In fact, I think it'd be better if you didn't.

**GREG**  That's kind of what we thought, too.

**SARAH**  Let me take care of it for you. It will be my last official duty.

**GREG**  Terrific. *(Rises, extends his hand.)* Well, Dean Daniels, I have to say, it's turned out to be a pleasure knowing you.

**SARAH**  And you. *(She shakes his hand.)* Good luck with everything.

**GREG**  You too. *(He starts to leave, stops.)* Could I . . .

**SARAH**  Yes?

**GREG**  I just wonder, could I ask you something about Simon Brick?

**SARAH**  Yes?

**GREG**  There's a rumor going around that he did this to himself.

**SARAH**  He did.

**GREG**  Wow. That's major. Do you know why he did it?

**SARAH**  I don't know.

GREG  Huh. You know, we talked about this a lot last night. About Simon. What if he was doing it to himself.

SARAH  And what did you conclude?

GREG  We didn't conclude anything. All we could do was guess. Simon wasn't there.

SARAH  Right.

GREG  In fact, we kept asking all the black people there, you know, why did he do it? And finally, this guy Jason said, "I don't know why he did it. It's not like we all think alike, just because we're black." You know? His whole point was that he wasn't the spokesperson for his race. He said, "That's just one of those things you white people assume about blacks. That we all think alike." But then this girl Lisa said, "But now you're saying that all *white* people think alike. How is that any different?" *(Laughs.)* We went around and around with that for an hour practically.

SARAH  It's hard, isn't it?

GREG  Yeah, it's hard. But I wouldn't say it was impossible. I guess that's what we realized last night.

SARAH  You're just starting, of course.

GREG  Oh, believe me, I'm not naïve enough to think we're all going to, you know, teach the world to sing. I just think it's important to try.

SARAH  To go out on a limb.

GREG  Exactly.

SARAH  *(Nods. Beat.)* All right, Greg. Good luck with the group.

GREG  Thanks a lot. Seriously. And good luck to you, too.

**SARAH** Thank you. *(He leaves.* SARAH *turns and walks to her windows. She looks outside. The sunlight is very bright. For a moment, she watches the campus. The chapel bells chime. It is one o'clock. She turns and goes to her phone. She picks up a file and opens it, checks a number, and dials. On phone)* Simon? . . . Hi. This is Dean Daniels calling. From Belmont . . . Hi. I just wanted to call and see if you were all right. *(Beat.)* Well, Mr. Meyers said when he dropped you off last night that your parents weren't home, so I just wanted to call and see if everything went all right with them. *(Beat.)* So were they mad? *(Beat.)* Oh Christ. Dean Kenney was supposed to call them. *(Beat.)* So they just came in and there you were? . . . What'd you do? *(She laughs.)* How'd they take that? *(She laughs again.)* Oh dear. Well, at least you have a sense of humor about it. That's a good sign, I think . . . Right. *(Beat.)* So how are you feeling today? *(Long pause. She listens.)* Oh, Simon. *(Pause.)* Listen, don't be so hard on yourself. Okay? *(Beat.)* Simon? *(Beat.)* Simon. It's okay. You hear me? Simon? *(Beat. Softly)* It's okay.